LEARNING FROM COUNTRY HOUSES

Christopher Culpin

The National Trust

Contents

Previous page: below stairs at Lanhydrock in Cornwall - a domestic service sign in the corridor (top left) and the Bake House (lower right).

Country houses are not just case-studies in architectural history. They are the stories of people's lives.

Take, for example, the dairy at Uppark in Sussex. Its cool tiled interior reflects the early nineteenth century's awareness of the need for cleanliness and hygiene in the days before refrigeration. The high quality of its decoration shows the interest that landowners of the period took in the running of their farms.

And it was here, in 1824, that the seventy-year-old Sir Harry Fetherstonhaugh proposed to his young dairymaid, Mary Ann Bullock. She was too surprised to speak. 'Don't answer me now,' said Sir Harry, 'but if you will have me, cut a slice out of the leg of mutton that is coming up for my dinner today.' When the mutton arrived, the slice was cut. The couple lived in quiet married seclusion until Sir Harry died in 1845, after which his widow ran Uppark until her own death in 1874.

It is not just the lives of the rich and powerful that we find out about when we visit a country house. We can see how their servants lived and worked. We can see the skill of the bricklayers and stonecarvers, the joiners and upholsterers who built and furnished it. Often we can visit not only the house, but other parts of the estate where different lives were led, learning about the blacksmith, the miller and the farmworker.

Sir Harry Fetherstonhaugh of Uppark.

History comes alive for children, and for many adults, when it is about people and how they lived their lives. People in the past demanded much the same things of their houses as we do. They wanted somewhere warm and dry to rest at the end of the day; somewhere to sleep, to cook, to eat and entertain guests. What is often so different is how they met those basic requirements. Whether we are looking at a fortified medieval castle or a baroque palace, whether a country house was built to impress royalty with its splendour or simply for friends to enjoy a weekend together, we find those similarities and intriguing differences which make history so fascinating.

Encounters with country houses can play an important part in National Curriculum History, as the 1995 Orders point out. At Key Stage 2 the Study Units on Life in Tudor Times, Victorian Britain and Local History are all particularly relevant, as are the Key Stage 3 Units on Medieval Realms, The Making of the United Kingdom and Britain 1750-1900. When they see how a country house and its estate were used, children discover something about the

The dairy at Uppark where Sir Harry proposed to his dairymaid.

lives of people in the past. But they find out about more than just the changing patterns of everyday life. In discovering why the hall of a medieval house was so large, why the home of a Georgian landowner is so full of references to ancient Greece and Rome or why kitchens and dining rooms in Victorian houses were so far apart, they are finding out about the attitudes, values and beliefs of the people who lived there. Their understanding of the past is deepened.

The National Trust

As the largest private conservation charity in the country, caring for more than two hundred country houses in England, Wales and Northern Ireland, the National Trust's educational policy is simple. Its four aims are: to help young people to enjoy and understand the coast, countryside and buildings in its care; to make young people aware of the Trust and its purposes; to encourage young people to help the Trust, both by becoming members and through practical voluntary work; and to extend its educational programme to older students and adult learners through working holidays, volunteering, vocational training and continuing education schemes.

Every year the National Trust welcomes well over half a million schoolchildren to its properties. It has been directly involved in all aspects of heritage education for more than two decades.

The Young National Trust Theatre in action - scholarly and exciting reconstructions of history.

• It runs an Education Group Membership scheme, a special category of Trust membership for schools and colleges. A yearly subscription enables Education Group Members to bring groups of up to sixty students to any Trust property - normal admission charges are waived.

• The Young National Trust Theatre is the Trust's own professional Theatre-in-Education company. It tours nine properties around the country every year, and around 7,000 children between the ages of eight and fourteen take part in the company's scholarly and exciting reconstructions of aspects of British history. Company members have skills in music, dance and teaching.

• Arts in Trust workshops regularly take place at different National Trust properties across the country. Writers, painters, sculptors and poets work closely with groups of schoolchildren, using an historic house or a beautiful landscape as a creative stimulus for work in Art and English.

• The National Trust also operates study bases at more than forty key properties that lend themselves particularly well to educational use. These bases are equipped with handling collections, field equipment, books and other study aids, enabling school groups to pursue in-depth work in History, Science and Geography.

• The Trust produces a wide range of teachers' resource books and other materials for properties which receive large numbers of school groups. These books offer practical and background information, primary sources, activities and ways of linking a visit with the National Curriculum.

Planning a Visit

Taking children out of school nowadays can be a complicated and expensive business. If it is going to be worth the effort and cost the visit must justify itself in the curriculum and the children should expect some educational benefit.

Preparation This has to be carefully gauged. Too much and the children are turned off before they even leave school; too little and they will miss the point of the visit. They should have some idea about the building styles of the period and about who lived in the house at that time.

The Mill at Cotehele in Cornwall. It is not only the rich and powerful that we learn about from a visit to a country house and its estate.

At the house A country house is a primary source, and like any primary source, it has to be interpreted. This is best achieved through active learning, so give the children things to do; but don't give them pointless tasks designed only to keep them busy. It is better to ask a few more demanding questions which make them look and think, than to provide dozens of 'fill-in-the-blanks' worksheets. At a house which is of several dates - and most are - focus their attention on the evidence of the period they are studying and relate evidence of other periods to that. Don't try to keep them constantly on task. Leave time for them to absorb the atmosphere.

Follow-up Apart from writing up the discoveries they made on the visit, this is the time to broaden the investigation. The house and its inhabitants can be put in a wider context. Links can be made with national history. Further sources can be introduced. Groups of pupils might follow up different aspects of the life and history of the house.

This book

The aim of this book is to provide enough information for teachers to be able to help pupils at Key Stages 2 and 3 to get the most out of a visit to a country house. It is divided into chapters based on the appropriate National Curriculum Study Units; the thrust of each chapter is on how houses were lived in and why people wanted them to look the way they do. Recurring themes include food and drink, leisure, change and continuity, servants and interior decoration; and there are suggestions for the kind of question you might ask pupils to think about in different parts of the house.

There are also four separate investigations which examine how particular types of historical source can be used to find out more about country houses.

The key to William the Conqueror's success in subduing England so effectively lay in building castles, safe bases from which Norman lords could control the neighbourhood. Hundreds of motte and bailey castles were put up, first in wood, then later in stone, as design changed to keep pace with developments in warfare.

Over the next four centuries there were occasional civil wars, but many castles never saw battle at all. Nevertheless, they remained the power-bases of the people who ruled the country. Who lived in them?

The answer is - at times a lot of people, mainly men. Most great medieval lords owned several estates and journeyed regularly between them. For months on end a castle would be almost empty, with just benches and trestles lining the bare walls. Then a huge procession would arrive. Packhorses and wagons would be unloaded. Hangings, cushions, tools, tablecloths, musical instruments, clothes, linen, pots, pans and spits were brought in. And a hundred or more servants would fill the castle with noise.

The Medieval Household

First, there were those who helped run the lord's estates: a steward, with his gown and staff, and educated clerks to do the accounts. Then there was a fighting force of soldiers, about half the total number in the household. These men wore the badge of their lord, his 'livery'. If serious numbers of fighting men were needed the lord could call on his retainers, also wearers of his livery but not permanent members of the household, who would turn out with soldiers of their own.

These fighting men were obviously the basis of a lord's power and prestige, although that power and prestige were also upheld by the rituals which surrounded a lord and lady in their daily lives. Servants attended them from the moment they woke until the moment they went to bed. They were waited on at meals by teams of attendants on bended knee. They had their own priest to celebrate mass in the chapel.

All the lord's close attendants were gentlemen, not lowly servants. Henry II's eldest son served in Thomas Becket's household; Thomas More, son of a Justice of the King's Bench, served in the household

---

Breakfast for Thirty

Meals: Breakfast for 30, dinner for 160, supper for 30.

Pantry: 314 white and 40 black loaves, wine and ales.

Kitchen: 2 pigs, 2 swans, 12 geese, 2 sheep, 24 chickens, 17 rabbits.

Source 1. From the **Account Book of Lady Alice de Brienne for New Year's Day** (1413).

---

of Bishop Morton. These young men, sent into a great household from the age of about seven, gained experience, education and contacts in the wider world. Their lord benefited from their abilities and the prestige of having such distinguished men serving him. And each of these gentlemen or yeomen would have one or more servants of their own.

One of the reasons for so many servants was that the sheer size of a household reflected the prestige of a lord. Lavish hospitality was expected (Source 1). At big feasts like New Year, there were many guests. Enormous quantities of food were prepared and the leftovers given away.

The castle buildings had to express all this power, ritual, wealth and hospitality.

Source 2. Monasteries were another kind of huge household. Here at Fountains Abbey in Yorkshire there were 50-100 monks and perhaps 500 lay-brothers. The monastery also had a duty of hospitality to all travellers.

Source 4. A lord and his lady, from a 15th-century manuscript.

Source 3. Bodiam Castle, East Sussex - a local powerbase.

Ideas

- In 1512 The Earl of Northumberland still kept a very medieval household, with 9 women and 157 men. Why was the ratio of women to men unbalanced in this way?

- What effect would it have on life in the household?

- Ask pupils to imagine the scene at a castle at the moment when a lord, lady and all their retinue and baggage arrives. What would they see? What would they hear?

Bodiam Castle, East Sussex

Bodiam Castle was built in the 1380s for Sir Edward Dalyngrigge, a soldier who had fought in France in the Hundred Years' War. The castle is both a grand residence and a response to the threat of a French invasion. This drawing shows the castle as it might have appeared around 1400. Dalyngrigge's private rooms and the chapel were in the east range and the south-east tower. The Great Hall and the kitchens filled the south range. As if to emphasise Bodiam's dual role, there was a separate hall and kitchen for garrison personnel in the west range.

Ideas

- How did people get into the castle? How could this entry be cut off? What other defensive features can pupils see in this drawing?

- How is the castle made to look imposing and important?

N

Great Hall

Kitchen

Solar

Retainers' Hall

Retainers' Kitchen

Gatchouse

Barbican

Eating in the Hall

The centre of the life of the household in the early Middle Ages was the great hall, where the lord and lady sat down to eat with all the members of their household. (They called them their 'family'.) Sources 1 and 3 explain the hall's importance. This is the ideal picture of the medieval household, with its sense of community, an ideal which lasted long after people had ceased to live like that. Even when the hall was no longer used on a daily basis, the whole household would gather there for great celebrations.

To seat all the household, and to express the importance of the lord, halls were both wide and high. Roofing them was a challenge to medieval designers. Their different solutions combine engineering skill, carpentry and beauty to an impressive degree.

The usual layout of the hall was that the lord, lady and important guests sat at a table across one end. Its significance was marked out in a number of ways: it might be raised on a dais (literally a 'high table'); there might be a canopy over it; it might be well-lit with a specially large window. In early medieval halls the fire was in the middle of the floor, but by the fourteenth century wall fireplaces were built to warm those sitting at high table. The lord or lady would have what was often the only chair in the whole building. Honoured guests and close members of the family sat on stools. Everyone else sat on benches at long trestle tables, usually on the outside only so that they could be served easily and could see everyone else.

At the lower end of the hall, the end furthest away from the high table, were the outside doors with a screen to keep out draughts. Beyond the screen were three doors facing the lord. The central one led to the kitchen, the others to the buttery (from the French *bouteillerie*), where beer, wine and cider were stored, and the pantry (French *paneterie*) where bread was stored.

Mealtimes

Meals in the great hall followed an elaborate ritual, designed to enhance the position of the head of the household. Grooms of the hall would set up the tables. The head of the household's place was set with a roll of white bread wrapped in a napkin.

Then came the gentleman carver. In some households, one of his tasks was to cut large slices of four-day-old bread into trenchers to act as plates; in others, bread was baked into special flat loaves which were used as trenchers. The gentleman sewer took *sayes* or samples, to check that everything was acceptable. He then went to the kitchens to collect the food. This was carried in grand procession into the hall. Trumpets sounded and everyone took off their hats. Principal guests washed their hands and were seated in strict order of seniority. And the meal began.

The carver cut the meat into slices. The server arranged helpings in groups, called *messes* (hence the word 'messmates'). Important people got a whole mess to themselves. Leftovers went to the side tables and then to the poor.

Cracking of Trumpets

[They] dined on the dais and daintily fared
And many a trusty man below at the long tables
Then forth came the first course with cracking of trumpets
On which many bright banners bravely were hanging
Noise of drums then anew, and the noble pipes
Warbling wild and keen, wakened their music
So that men's hearts rose high hearing their playing.

Source 1. From **The Romance of Sir Gawain and the Green Knight** *(mid-14th century).*

Source 2. The Great Hall at Lytes Cary in Somerset.

The High Board

Make your own household sit in the hall as much as you may and sit you ever in the middle of the high board that your visage and cheer be showed to all men.

Source 3. Bishop Grosseteste's advice to the Countess of Lincoln (late 13th century).

Ideas

- In a medieval great hall, ask pupils to look at the roof. How is the weight carried to the walls? How does the structure resist the tendency to splay out? How does it resist pressure to fall sideways? Is all the wood necessary or is some decorative? Are some timbers both?

- Ask pupils to explore the end of the hall where the head of the household sat. How is it marked off as being more important? Is there a dais, a window, a canopy of state, a fireplace?

- Ask pupils to investigate the lower end of the hall. Find the main entrance door. How is it screened off? How many other doors lead off the hall at this end? Where did they go? Where do they go now?

- In class, your pupils might try role-playing a medieval feast. Roles will include the lord and lady of the house and important guests - noblemen, bishops, abbesses etc; upper servants, such as the yeomen of the buttery and pantry, the gentleman carver and gentleman sewer; and grooms of the hall. Props might include goblets, trenchers, jugs, a basin and towels, knives, spoons and napkins. As well as marking out an area for the great hall, you'll need two other rooms 'off' - a kitchen and a chamber where the guests wait to be called in.

Source 4. Great Chalfield Manor, Wiltshire - looking towards the screens at the lower end of the Hall.

Source 5. An artist's impression of a feast in the Great Hall at Penshurst Place, Kent.

Chambers and Solars

The ideal of the whole household eating together in the great hall was fine in theory, but from the middle of the fourteenth century the lord began to eat elsewhere. William Langland, writing in 1362, laments the change, as Source 1 shows. The whole household might feast together on special occasions, but these were increasingly rare.

So where did the lord go, and why? Many castles and houses have a room called a great chamber. This was originally the main sleeping area of the head of the household, and usually on the first floor. Here, in a warmer, smaller, better-lit room, the lord and his close family could eat their meals, not necessarily alone, but with much more privacy. This search for privacy, the desire to spend time in a room where one would not have to be constantly keeping up appearances under the gaze of every kitchen-boy and washerwoman, was to continue throughout history.

As the great chamber became the focus of ceremonial in the house, its importance increased. The procession carrying the food from the kitchen to the high table now went right through the hall and up the stairs. This meant building a more impressive staircase, and paying more attention to the decoration of the great chamber. An important feature was the window: being on the first floor the chamber could be much lighter than the hall, with a huge window - often an *oriel*, a window which projected out from the wall high up. For this reason the great chamber was sometimes called the *solar* - the sun-room.

The Parlour

As the great chamber was gradually drawn into the ceremony of the household, the lord and lady lost what they were originally looking for - privacy. And so another room came into use: the parlour (from the French *parler*, to talk). This tended to be placed behind the upper end of the hall, on the ground floor, often directly underneath the great chamber. It was comfortable and accessible, and had a low ceiling, so that it could be warmed more easily than the chamber above.

The north side of the hall court at Cotehele House in Cornwall, which was built between 1489 and 1520, tells this story clearly. The door in front of you in Source 4 leads into the hall, which extends to the left, including the large windows. Further to the left is the gabled crosswing, with the parlour on the ground floor and the solar on the first floor. Both parlour and solar have large south-facing windows. The solar has a commanding position at the centre of the life of the house. Small peep-holes allow the occupant to look down one way into the chapel and the other into the hall.

The Lord Deserts the Hall

Wretched is the hall...each day in the week
There the lord and lady liketh not to sit.
Now have the rich a rule to eat by themselves
In a privy parlour...for poor men's sake,
Or in a chamber with a chimney, and leave the chief hall
That was made for meals, for men to eat in.

Source 1. From **The Vision of Piers Plowman**, by William Langland (1362).

Source 2. The north front of Great Chalfield Manor; the Hall lies to the left of the entrance.

Ideas

- During a visit to a medieval country house, ask pupils to compare the great hall and the great chamber. They should think about *size* (which is the bigger of the two?); *heating* (which is easier to heat?); *privacy* (how did people get to each from outside?); and *impact* (which has the more impressive decoration, and which has the larger windows?).

- Why is William Langland (Source 1) sorry about changes in the use of the hall?

- Look at Sources 2 and 4. What clues are there that the high end of the hall is to the left in each case?

Source 3. Alfriston Clergy House, East Sussex. Built in the 14th century, probably for a well-to-do farmer, Alfriston is a good example of a smaller medieval house.

Source 4. Cotehele House, Cornwall - the Great Hall, with the Parlour Wing to the left.

13

Towers

By the fifteenth century the use of gunpowder and the relatively peaceful nature of English life had made castles almost redundant. Yet the castle as an obvious outward sign of wealth and power was still present in people's minds. And of all castle features it was the great keep - a concept which enjoyed its heyday in the mid-twelfth century - which attracted the fantasies of fifteenth-century builders.

Looking at Sources 1 and 2, Tattershall Castle in Lincolnshire, you can see why. It looms over the flat surrounding countryside, with turrets, machicolations, battlements and flagpoles like a picture in a medieval manuscript. In fact it would hardly have put off a determined gang of attackers for long. Its walls are made of brick, which would shatter on being hit by a cannonball, and its huge windows reach nearly to the ground. It is a parody of its twelfth-century model, Castle Hedingham in Essex.

When the tower was built (between 1430 and 1450 by Ralph, Lord Cromwell, Treasurer of England) there was a hall next to it. The tower provided the kind of accommodation this hall lacked - rooms for the household to sleep in and splendid private lodgings. The bottom floor was a basement, probably for servants to sleep in. It did not communicate with the next floor up, which was a parlour. This in turn did not communicate with the three top rooms, which were from the bottom up, another hall, a great chamber and a private bedchamber.

Oxburgh Hall in Norfolk, built in 1482, has a huge, impressive and equally out-of-time gatehouse (Source 3). This has grand rooms on two floors, the largest called the King's Room after a visit there by Henry VII in 1487. Other buildings around a courtyard provide all other necessary accommodation.

Source 1. Tattershall Castle, Lincolnshire, built in the mid-15th century.

Source 2. Tattershall in 1726, showing the remains of the buildings that once surrounded the tower.

Source 3. Oxburgh Hall, Norfolk, with its huge gatehouse.

Ideas

- Ask pupils to make a sketch of the basic outline of either Tattershall or the gatehouse at Oxburgh, and to turn it into a medieval fantasy by adding banners, shields, flags, and knights in armour.

- Both Tattershall and Oxburgh would be easy to attack. What features make them so vulnerable?

It seems likely that the hundred-plus members of early medieval households slept where they could. Straw pallets were rolled up during the day and put down at night. Some were as big as 9ft by 6ft, so presumably two or even three people slept on them. Kitchen boys, or scullions, slept on the floor of the kitchen; other servants slept on the hall floor; and others simply found nooks and crannies where they could. The close attendants of the lord and lady slept outside their chamber door or even, in early times, at the foot of their bed.

By the fourteenth century changes began to take place. Lodgings, sometimes no more than single rooms, were built or converted from existing buildings. Often they were grouped around a courtyard, with a door and staircase leading to a pair of rooms on each floor. These extra courtyards of lodgings increased the size of late medieval houses quite dramatically - good surviving examples can still be seen in Oxford and Cambridge colleges and in the early Tudor ranges at Hampton Court.

Beds were as simple and portable as benches and tables. They had a wooden frame with rope strung across it to hold the mattress. This was stuffed with straw or perhaps feathers, and covered with rugs or furs. Every so often the rope would have to be tightened to prevent the bed sagging - hence the expression 'Sleep tight'.

But beds were a luxury for the few. Most people in a country house had to make do with a mattress or a rug on the floor.

Ideas

* Where would the following people sleep in a medieval house? On what? And how comfortable do pupils think they would be?

  The lord and lady

  The lord's page

  The lady's gentlewoman servant

  An upper servant

  An upper servant's servant

  A groom of the hall

  A kitchen boy

A Good Night's Sleep

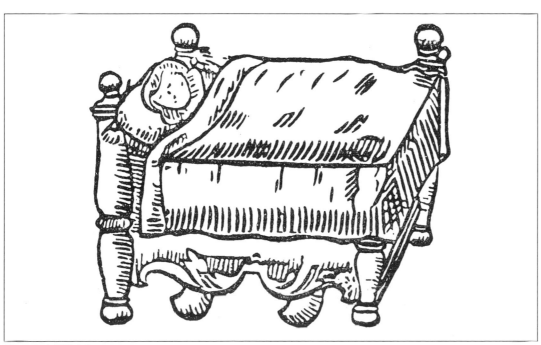

Source 1. A child's bed.

The Kitchens

We have already looked at the sheer size of medieval feasts. This meant, of course, that the medieval kitchen, the centre of the whole operation of preparing food, had to be large. These huge rooms can still be seen in castles, monasteries and medieval houses; the one at Fountains Abbey in Yorkshire is 50ft square. They were high too, to let the heat and fumes from the enormous fires escape upwards. The Abbot's Kitchen at Glastonbury Abbey, Somerset, is 41ft high.

Cooking hearths were equally gigantic. The main hearth at Compton Castle in Devon is 15ft across (Source 3). Heat was provided by wood or charcoal and food could be roasted, boiled or baked.

Roasted meat was the centrepiece of medieval cooking. This was done on a spit, turned to ensure it was evenly cooked on all sides by a small boy, a turnspit, who spent most of his life in the kitchen, sleeping there and scarcely ever venturing into the rest of the house. Whole animals or birds or fish could be roasted in this way, or divided into joints.

Often food was boiled or stewed. *Pottage*, halfway between a soup and a stew, was the common dish at all levels of society. Cauldrons or kettles were placed over or hung over a fire; meat, fish and vegetables were slowly stewed; and the mixture was thickened with grain or breadcrumbs.

Source 3 shows the bread oven at the right hand side of the main hearth. This was heated by placing burning faggots of wood inside. When the correct temperature was reached - largely a matter of guesswork - the ashes were swept out and the oven was ready. Bread was baked first, when the oven was hottest, then pies and tarts, then small cakes. The tops of tarts and flans could be browned using a *salamander*, a solid flat piece of metal, heated in the open hearth and then passed over the top of the dish.

Menus

A medieval feast was served up in a way quite unlike the order of dishes that western cultures are familiar with today. A course, or mixture of dishes, was served at once, followed by a second 'course' or different mixture - in much the same way that a Chinese meal is served. Many dishes were quite sophisticated, requiring the use of exotic spices.

Roast meat was usually served with a sauce (in a saucer) into which the meat was dipped. On special occasions a third course, called a *banquet*, might also be served.

Showpiece dishes were expected at great feasts, and the showiest of all was the 'peacock in his hackle'. A peacock was carefully skinned, stuffed and roasted, with the head wrapped in damp cloth to prevent it cooking. It was then cooled, the skin sewn on, the beak and feet decorated with gold, the tail feathers spread out and a wad of spirit-soaked wool put in its mouth, set alight as the bird arrived at table.

Other spectacular dishes, called *subtleties*, were made of marzipan or pastry, shaped and coloured. Often the aim was to present an appropriate design as a tribute to an honoured guest - a coat of arms, a heraldic beast or statue.

Source 1. The kitchen fireplace at Bodiam Castle.

Hooks and Hatchets

In a kitchen there should be a small table for shredding vegetables, pods, tripods, a pestle and mortar, a hatchet, a stirring stick, a hook, a cauldron, a bronze vessel, small pitchers, a bowl, a platter, a pickling vat and knives for cleaning fish... The chief cook should have a cupboard for aromatic spices and sifted bread flour.

Source 2. Adapted from a 12th-century account.

Source 3. The medieval kitchen at Compton Castle, Devon.

Flampoyntes of Cream

FIRST COURSE

Boar's head

Bruet of almayne to pottage [a stew of rabbit, flavoured with almond, ginger, and rice-flour and coloured red]

Baked teal and woodcock

Pheasants and curlews

SECOND COURSE

Partridge and mallard

Pottage of minced chicken, ground almonds and white wine

Cawdel ferry [wine, sweetened and thickened, with saffron and egg yolks]

Flampoyntes of cream and tarts [open tarts of minced pork and cheese]

THIRD COURSE

Plovers, larks and stuffed chicken

Mawmenny [pottage of minced chicken with sweetened wine, pine nuts, dates and spices]

Source 4. Adapted from a roll of recipes of around 1390.

Ideas

- In a medieval kitchen, ask pupils the following questions:

  Where is cooking done? Where is food prepared?

  What different cooking methods were used here? Look for ovens, spits, cauldrons and racks to hold them.

  Where is the water supply?

  Where was the salt kept dry?

  What storage space for ingredients is there?

  How many things from Source 2 can you see?

  What evidence is there that this kitchen prepared large amounts of food?

- What was it like to work in the medieval kitchen? How did the smoke and heat escape, and where did the light come from?

- In what ways did a medieval master cook need skills that a modern master chef does not need? Pupils might write a job description, saying what they expect the cook to do and describing the facilities their imaginary medieval kitchen contains.

Water

Medieval castles, monasteries and country houses needed a good supply of water for cooking and washing. Even though they did not know why, medieval people were aware that cleanliness kept disease at bay and that flowing water was necessary for washing away waste. The medieval monastery of Fountains was strategically sited on the River Skell, which flows right through the site. The buildings of the monastery were arranged so that its waters arrived pure for the monks to wash; it then flowed past the kitchen in pipes of wood or lead, and finally was used to flush the privies.

Such arrangements required considerable design skills. They were often found in monasteries, but it is not true to say that everyone else lived in total squalor. Royal palaces had running water from the twelfth century, and by the 1300s royal bathrooms were provided with hot and cold running water of a sort.

However, medieval castle and house builders did not give a fresh water supply the priority that monks did. This was partly a matter of defence - it was not possible to build a castle with a stream flowing through it in the way that it did at Fountains Abbey. Most castles had to rely on wells within the walls - at Bodiam there is a well 8ft in diameter and 11ft deep next to the kitchen (Source 1). Castles and houses on hills had even greater problems in laying on water supplies, and some had to rely on collecting rainwater in great cisterns.

The moat certainly could not be used - it was primarily a place for the disposal of sewage. At Baddesley Clinton in Warwickshire, for example, there is a drain running along one side into which all the privies and other waste water fell or flowed. Slits in the wall allowed the moat water to wash out this drain (Source 3).

Castles often had elaborate systems of *garderobes* or privies (Source 4). By the later Middle Ages, lodgings were arranged all round the building, each with its own privy. (Bodiam has more than thirty.) These were specially built in the thickness of the walls of towers or turrets. Shafts carried away their contents, perhaps into the moat if there was one, or simply out onto the hillside if there wasn't. Some shafts were simply blocked at the bottom and had to be cleared out each year.

Drink

The one thing not to do with water in the Middle Ages was to drink it. Every medieval household of any size, not just castles and palaces, had its own brewhouse. Most people drank a weak brew of fermented barley called *ale*. Because it did not keep very well and soon tasted quite sour, it was often flavoured with herbs or spices. Ale was drunk at all meals, including breakfast. It was served from huge leather jugs called jacks.

In the fifteenth century some brewers began to make beer flavoured with hops. Although like most new tastes, it had its opponents (Source 2), the hops did improve its keeping qualities. By then most large households were only brewing twice a year, in March and October.

In the south and west most people drank cider. A cider-house still survives at Buckland Abbey in Devon. At Cotehele in Cornwall, there is cider-making equipment, including a donkey-powered apple-crusher. It dates only from the nineteenth century, but the technology was much the same as in medieval times. Cider was made from crab-apples as well as cider-apples; another popular drink was *perry*, made from pears. Wine was only drunk by the rich. A few monasteries had vineyards, but most wine was imported.

Ideas

- How was the medieval house or castle you are visiting supplied with water?

- Where did the waste water go?

- What lavatory arrangements were there, and what evidence of them can pupils find?

- Can pupils see any evidence of brewing at the house?

- Medieval people did not know about germs, but they knew that dirty water could make them ill. How did they know this? And how did this knowledge affect the design of castles and country houses, and the things that people ate and drank?

Source 1. The well in the south-west tower of Bodiam Castle.

Beer Makes a Man Fat

[Beer is] a Dutch boorish liquor, a thing not known in England till of late days, to the detriment of many Englishmen, for the drink is a cold drink; yet it doth make a man fat and doth inflate the belly.

Source 2. From *A Compendyous Regyment or A Dyettary of Helth*, by Andrew Boorde (1542).

Source 3. Projecting privy block at Baddesley Clinton, Warwickshire.

Source 4. Castles often had elaborate systems of privies.

Investigating Inventories

How interesting it would be to see a country house just as it was when it was first built. Sometimes the National Trust is able to arrange rooms as they were, perhaps even using the original furniture. But in practice this is very difficult - furnishings and pictures have often been lost or sold or replaced with something more 'modern' over the centuries, just as the contents of our own homes tend to change through time.

Inventories allow us to find out exactly what furniture, objects and fabrics there were in the rooms at the moment the occupant died. They are properly called *probate inventories* and were attached to wills, listing and valuing every item of goods or furniture in the deceased's home. Before 1858, wills were proved in the church courts, so probate inventories are sometimes found in diocesan record offices, although many are now in county record offices. Some have been copied and printed.

A poor person's inventory might be a page or two long, listing only a few shabby home-made bits of furniture. But country house inventories can sometimes be very detailed and very long: the 1710 inventory of Dyrham Park in Avon runs to 39 pages and includes items from all over the world.

Inventories can help us answer that question we always ask: 'What was it like to live here?' The 1601 inventory from Hardwick Hall in Derbyshire tells us a great deal about how its owner, Bess of Hardwick, used the house. For example, she wrote her letters in her private bedchamber, where there were three desks. She tried to keep the notorious cold of Hardwick at bay with an enormous number of curtains, hangings and carpets, including eight mats around her bed. There were no garderobes at Hardwick: everyone used close-stools which were usually stored in closets, small rooms leading off the bedchambers. There were no clocks in Bess's chamber, but she had an hourglass. There were very few chairs, even in the Low Great Chamber, which was used as a private dining room. An effort was made to deal with smells around the house: there are numerous sweetbags and several dishes for burning scented pastilles.

The Dyrham inventory of 1710, signed by the housekeeper, Sarah Saunders, shows how life had changed in just over 100 years. There are, for example, several clocks, over 300 chairs, 343 paintings and over 200 prints; there are items from India, Japan (or British-made copies of Japanese products) and lots of Delftware from Holland.

Using an Inventory

Work on a large inventory can be divided among the class. They will need a good glossary and some pictures of some of the more obscure items mentioned.

The 'sea-dog' table at Hardwick Hall. Mentioned in an inventory of 1601, it still stands in the house today.

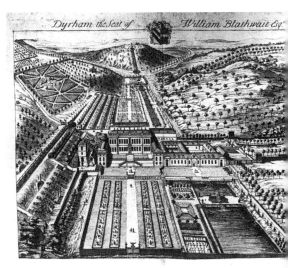

Dyrham Park, Avon. The 1710 inventory lists items from all over the world.

Before the Visit

(You could try to apply these ideas to the Dyrham Inventory extract opposite.)

- Make sure you understand what all the items are.
- What were they used for? How were they used?
- What were they made of?
- What does the document tell you about how the room was lit?
- What does it tell you about how the room was heated?
- What does it tell you about the importance of the room?
- What does it tell you about what kinds of things went on in the room?
- What differences are there between the kind of things we put in a room like this now and the things they had?
- How would you arrange these items in the room?

After the Visit

- What differences are there between how the room looks now and what was in the inventory?
- Was it arranged in the way you expected?
- How do the items in the inventory reflect the life-style of the occupants of the house?

The state bed at Dyrham. 'What does it tell you about the importance of the room?'

Here is the inventory for two rooms at Dyrham House in 1710:

The Family Parlour
6 cane chairs
a black leather couch
a table, pair of stands and a looking glass
a writing desk with drawers
a clock and a weather glass
a double grate and fender
a fire shovel, tongs, poker, brush and pair of bellows
5 pictures
3 blue window curtains
a small japan oval table

In the Terrace bedchamber:
an Indian calico bed
a feather bed, bolster and underquilt
a counterpane
4 pieces of hangings
a white fustian covering quilt
2 window curtains and valence of calico
4 elbow chairs, Irish stitch, with white painted calico covers
1 Dutch chair & 2 stools with green silk covers; 2 cushions
a looking glass
a Japan table and pair of stands with leather covers
a pair of Japan sconces
4 pictures
a Delft flower pot in the chimney

Glossary

Calico: a plain cotton cloth, made in India until its import was banned in 1701.
Elbow chair: high-backed upright chair with arms.
Fustian: a cloth woven from linen and cotton.
Irish stitch: a needlework stitch, the upright stitches worked in zig zag rows.
Japan: lacquered and not necessarily made in Japan - imitation Japan furniture was made in several places in Britain.
Sconce: a plate fixed to the wall with one or more branches to hold candles.
Stand: a candlestand.
Valence: a strip of fabric fitted to the top of a curtain.
Weather-glass: a barometer.

Visiting a Tudor Country House

Once you passed through the front door of a Tudor country house, you would find yourself in a short passage, with several doorways leading off to either side. The first main room you came to would be the great hall, still large and impressive in Tudor times (Source 1), but not as important as it had been when the whole household ate there together. As we saw in the last chapter, towards the end of the medieval period the owners of the house, wanting more privacy and comfort, stopped taking their meals in the hall. Although the servants still ate there, it was becoming a grand entrance where people waited to be shown into the presence of the owner. Only on special occasions, like Christmas, would everyone sit down here to a feast as they had in the old days.

But the hall still had to be grand, so that waiting visitors felt they were in the house of someone really important.

The Great Chamber

If you were a person of consequence, you would be shown up the main staircase - imposing in itself, since it was part of the processional route (Source 2) - to the great chamber. This was likely to be the grandest room in the house. It was usually on the first floor, away from the smells of the kitchen and the company of the lower servants. If the house did not have its own chapel, prayers were said here. The owner would receive visitors and eat in state here, with dishes carried ceremonially up from the kitchens. Afterwards the tables were cleared away and the company settled down to music, card games, plays or masques. In Shakespeare's *A Midsummer Night's Dream*, the play put on by the craftsmen is performed in the great chamber of the Duke of Athens.

As the Tudor dynasty established itself, the country became increasingly peaceful and prosperous, and the need to fortify houses grew less. The great chamber could be fitted with large windows, giving light and a view of the gardens. Perhaps stained-glass coats of arms would remind visitors how important and well-connected were the people in this house.

Tudor owners embellished their great chambers in new and fashionable ways. Renaissance themes, classical details and stories from ancient Rome and Greece could all appear. Fireplaces were adorned with large overmantels and chimneypieces. Walls were covered with panelling or tapestries. Plaster friezes and moulded plaster ceilings gave opportunities to include coats of arms, badges and other devices. All these had the effect of impressing the visitor with the power and prestige of the owner, while bringing in new standards of comfort (Source 3).

Ideas

During a visit to a Tudor country house, ask your pupils to answer the following questions.

- What do you think of the great hall? Is it an impressive room? How is the effect achieved? Look out for coats of arms, portraits, fine decoration, powerful features such as pillars and panelling. Is it a comfortable room?

- How wide is the staircase? How many people could walk up side by side? What impressive features can you see?

- What are your first impressions of the great chamber? Power? Wealth? Comfort? Formality? What words would you use?

- How has the fireplace been decorated? Is it the central feature of the room? Is there panelling? Is it plain or decorated? Are there tapestries, and if so, were they made for this room or cut to fit? What stories do the tapestries tell?

- Is there a moulded plaster frieze? What designs are used? Is the ceiling plastered? What patterns are used?

Source 1. The Tudor Great Hall at Rufford Old Hall, Lancashire - still large and impressive.

Source 2. Hardwick Hall, Derbyshire - the staircase was now part of the processional route.

Source 3. The High Great Chamber at Hardwick.

Who Lived in Tudor Houses?

Who lived in Tudor country houses? The answer is - lots of people. Tudor households, like medieval households, could be very large indeed. In the 1580s, for example, the Earl of Derby had a household of 115 to 140 people, although the norm was much smaller, perhaps between thirty and fifty. They ranged in rank from the upper servants who helped the lord or lady run their business, down to the lowest kitchenboy.

Strict order was kept. At Knole in Kent in the years 1613-24 (just outside the Tudor period, but still typical of the previous century) this order could be told from where people ate. The family dined in the great chamber; twenty upper servants, including the chaplain, the steward and the gentleman of the horse ate in the parlour. At the top table in the hall were the rest of the upper servants, such as the clerk of the kitchen, the yeomen of the buttery and pantry, baker, brewer and so on. At the long table below them sat lower servants: grooms, farriers, falconers, huntsmen and 'Solomon the bird-catcher'. There was a nursery table and a laundrymaids' table, with the few women servants, and finally one for the kitchens.

Why So Many?

Keeping a large household upheld the prestige of a great lord or lady. Every moment of the day was filled with ceremonies demanding the attendance of teams of servants. Many of these servants were themselves from families of some rank.

Bess of Hardwick (Source 3) served in the houses of the Zouche family, where she met her first husband, and the Greys. The young person would learn something of the world and make connections, while the household gained prestige from their presence.

The household also included men who wore the lord's 'livery', his badge or colours (Source 2), just as they had in medieval times. Henry VIII and Elizabeth I tried to cut down on the numbers of people in livery, seeing private armies as a threat to royal power. They were particularly worried when JPs wore the livery of their lord: what about independent justice?

So many servants meant that the household got through enormous amounts of food and drink (Source 1). Great lords and ladies were also expected to put on tremendous hospitality on big occasions. At the funeral of the 5th Earl of Shrewsbury in 1560, for example, 1200 people were fed, after which the leftovers and 2d. each (just under 1p) were given to the poor.

All these people had to live somewhere, of course. Many late medieval and early Tudor houses looked like Knole (Source 4). Vita Sackville-West, who lived there in the early twentieth century, described it as 'like a medieval village with no attempt at symmetry.' The house was taken over by Henry VIII who enlarged it by building an extra courtyard to provide rooms for his household. Thomas Sackville, 1st Earl of Dorset, became the owner of Knole in 1566 and added the curved gables at the beginning of the seventeenth century.

Shopping List

Provisions for a week:
an ox, 5 sheep, a calf a deer, a lamb,
wheat 16 bushels, malt 22 bushels,
oats 24 bushels, cheeses 3, sweet butter 2
dishes, and 7 of salt, butter, 4 geese, 3 pigs,
11 capons, and a hen, 26 coneys, 5 ducks,
11 teals, 6 woodcock, 5 partridges,
1 pheasant, 33 eggs
Purchases for a week:
24 plaice, 25 whiting, 3 pecks of
oysters, white and red herrings,
12 teal, 4 woodcock, 2 ducks and a widgeon
half a dish of butter, milk and cream

Source 1. From the Petre family account books of Ingatestone Hall, Essex (1552).

Breeches of Red Velvet

The Earl of Arundel entered all in gilt and engraved armour, with 4 pages and 22 gentlemen all dressed in cloaks and breeches of red velvet, with yellow feathers and yellow silk stockings. He had 6 trumpeters that sounded before him and 32 yeomen that waited after him, all in red and yellow.

Source 2. Description of the Earl of Arundel at a tournament (1581).

Source 3. Bess of Hardwick met her first husband while she was in service.

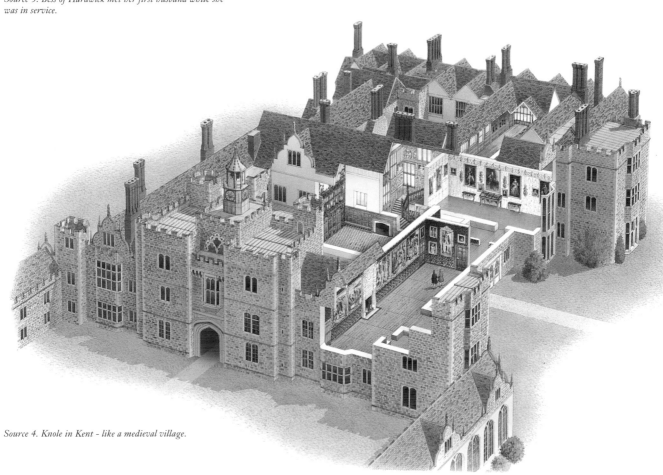

Source 4. Knole in Kent - like a medieval village.

Change and Continuity

For most of the Tudor period, country houses showed a good deal of continuity with the Middle Ages. There were still great halls, great chambers and parlours; sprawling courtyards still provided accommodation for large households. Yet there were important changes: exterior symmetry was much more important, for example, and cheaper glass and more sophisticated construction techniques meant that windows were often much bigger.

Ask pupils to look at the pictures on this page, identifying the significant features of each house and comparing the differences.

*Source 1. **Melford Hall, Suffolk**. Melford Hall was built some time between 1554 and 1578. Symmetrical, incorporating a sort of gatehouse, with 'pepper-pot' turrets, it was built by William Cordell who, like many Tudor housebuilders, was a rich lawyer of relatively humble origins.*

*Source 2. **Little Moreton Hall, Cheshire**. At the core of Little Moreton there is a hall of 1450 and two wings of 1480. From 1559 to 1570 a large new south block with extra lodgings for visitors and a long gallery were added. The effect of the two bays shown here is to add a great deal more light to the hall (left) and the parlour (right).*

Ideas

- Is the Tudor house your pupils are studying symmetrical? Does it have any military features? Would they serve any purpose in real sixteenth-century warfare?

- Are there any Renaissance ideas or motifs on the house?

- Are the windows original? What is their importance to the overall design?

- Does the house have an 'old-fashioned', medieval feel to it, or a 'modern', Tudor look? Is it more representative of change or continuity?

*Source 3. **The Gatehouse to Charlecote Park, Warwickshire**. A gatehouse, with portcullis and murder-holes, is a military building. The gatehouse at Charlecote, built about 1558, has no military use. Only the idea remains.*

*Source 4. **Knole, Kent**. Archbishop Bourchier of Canterbury owned Knole from 1456 until his death in 1486. He is thus almost outside the Tudor period. However, look at the picture, ignoring the bay windows (early17th century) and the clock tower (18th century). Does it show a castle? Hardly. It would not be able to withstand a determined assault from a few armed men, especially if any of them had firearms or cannon. There are too many windows, too low; the large and beautiful window in the tower makes it impossible to use the machicolations on the tower for assaulting attackers. Castles by now were for giving an impression of power, not for war.*

*Source 5. **Speke Hall, Merseyside**. Speke Hall was built and added to over three generations of the Norris family from the late 15th century to the early 17th century.*

Cooking and Eating

A meal in a great Tudor house normally consisted of two courses - each of up to thirty dishes. Storing, preparing and cooking such quantities of food must have been an enormous task.

One of the most important servants in the house was the clerk of the kitchen. He was responsible for: the granary; the cellar; the buttery; the larders, one for fish and meat, either fresh or cured, and one for dairy produce; the pantry, mainly for bread; the ewery for linen and candlesticks; the scullery for washing up; and the woodyard.

Tudor kitchens were not as big as their medieval predecessors, and were now rarely put in a separate building, but they were still large, high rooms. The main features were the great wide hearths, fired with wood. Ash was preferred for roasting, beech for boiling and cherrywood for the baking ovens.

Joints of meat, whole animals and fish were roasted on spits, turned to ensure they were evenly cooked. In Tudor times this was often done by dogs, walking round a treadwheel: special dogs with long bodies and short legs were bred for the task. Pottages were still boiled in huge cauldrons with vegetables and flavourings. Beehive ovens were fired with faggots of wood, which were then raked out and the food cooked while the ovens were still hot. Pies, often with elaborately decorated crusts, were very popular.

All these forms of cooking were quite crudely controlled, by moving the food nearer to or further from the heat. The skill of the cooks in making their kitchens work must have been considerable. As part of the growing sophistication of Tudor times, they were also called upon to create more complicated dishes. *Fricassees* involved frying small pieces of meat in butter, then stewing them in wine; *hashes* were dishes made with thin slices of meat. The cook's last job was to make sure that all the dishes were set out in the correct order on the servery.

Eating

The whole elaborate medieval ritual of serving meals to the great lord or lady continued into the Tudor period. First, the gentleman usher assembled with the yeomen of the ewery, pantry, buttery and cellar at around 10am, for dinner at 11am. The yeoman of the ewery prepared his basin, jug and fine damask towels on a board at the side. The cloth was

Source 1. Pomegranates on the ceiling of the Parlour at Speke Hall.

then carefully and ceremoniously laid and the great salt, the largest and most valuable piece of tableware, was put in position. The yeoman of the pantry set places for each diner, with trencher, napkin, knife and spoon. The gentleman usher then checked that the meal was ready and informed the host. The yeoman of the ewery took rose-scented water to the guests, with a jug, basin and towel, so that they could wash before sitting down. The carver and the sewer (server) also washed their hands and went with their helpers to the serving table outside the kitchen, where the food was laid out. The food was then taken in procession from there to the great chamber. All present stood to attention with hats off. The gentleman usher led the sewer to the table, where the dishes were laid out in symmetrical patterns. Any meat to be carved was given to the carver, and the gentlemen of the chamber acted as waiters.

Good Table Manners

For rudeness it is thy pottage to sup
Or speak to any, his head in the cup.
Thy knife see be sharp to cut fair thy meat;
Thy mouth not too full when thou dost eat;
Not smacking thy lips, as commonly do hogs,
Pick not thy teeth at the table sitting,
Nor use at thy meat over-much spitting;
This rudeness if youth is to be abhorred;
Thyself mannerly behave at the board.

*Source 2. From **The Schoole of Vertue and Booke of Goode Nouture of Chyldren**, by Francis Seager (1557).*

We have already seen that great chambers were more luxuriously decorated than medieval halls. It was the fashion to cover tables with carpets from the east (Source 4). Plasterwork designs might reflect how the room was used; so, for example, at Speke Hall it includes grapes (Source 1) as well as pomegranates and hazelnuts.

Many houses still did not provide guests with knives. Clearly the author of Source 2 expected you to bring your own. Forks were just coming into fashion. Spoons were provided: Bess of Hardwick had '31 gilt spoons and 36 other spoons whereof 11 are with knobs and 9 with the apostles'. Pewter was starting to appear in place of wooden plates, one of the many signs of the higher standard of living enjoyed in Tudor times.

Source 2 can be taken as a sign of greater sophistication, greater awareness of manners. It suggests that medieval table manners could often be rather gross. Or perhaps such rules were only necessary because Tudor table manners were not very refined.

Source 3. The Tudor kitchen at Buckland Abbey, Devon.

Ideas

- Act out a visit to a Tudor mansion. A party of five or six guests arrive at the house and are shown into the great hall. Some servants are also in the hall, or are passing through on their tasks. The guests discuss what they can see.

  They are then shown up to the great chamber, where the host and hostess welcome them and point out features of the room. They all go up to the long gallery while the great chamber is prepared for dinner. The gentleman usher and the yeomen of the ewery, pantry, buttery and cellar go about their work with the carver and other gentlemen of the chamber. The meal is set out and served. Music is provided during the pauses between courses.

Source 4. East Riddlesden Hall, Yorkshire - it was the fashion to cover a table with a carpet.

Long Galleries

Galleries were used in medieval times to connect rooms. Sometimes they were on two, three or four sides of a house, and on two floors. They were often open on one side. What was new in Tudor times was the idea that these galleries should be used for pleasure and recreation, rather than just to get from one room to another. The Long Gallery at The Vyne in Hampshire was one of the earliest to be used in this way (Source 1). By Elizabeth's reign, long galleries were being built for their own sake, not leading anywhere but part of the state rooms of the house. Builders vied with each other to create the longest, broadest and most magnificent.

They were primarily used for indoor exercise. Tudor doctors were always emphasising daily exercise and, in the British climate, the long gallery made this possible. They were also used for games - a Tudor tennis-ball was found behind a panel in the gallery at Little Moreton Hall (Source 2), and the gallery at Ingatestone Hall contained a shovelboard 14ft long.

Galleries were also convenient places for musical entertainments and plays. The growth of companies of travelling players in this period is evidence of the interest in this kind of entertainment.

At first, long galleries had bare walls. But over the years, owners came to realise that they were suitable places to display pictures. They might hang portraits of family connections, or of living statesmen and courtiers - the Tudor equivalent of signed photographs.

Source 2. A tennis ball was found behind the panelling in the Gallery at Little Moreton Hall.

Ideas

- During your visit to a Tudor country house, ask pupils to look at the long gallery. How long do they think it is? How wide? Is there a good view from the windows?

- How does the gallery relate to the great chamber? Is it on the same floor? If not, are the stairs clearly part of the grand route?

- Are there portraits? Of whom? What are they trying to say about the owners of this house?

Source 1. The Long Gallery at The Vyne, Hampshire.

Source 1. Banqueting Room in the tower at Lacock Abbey, Wiltshire.

When a dinner was over the servants cleared the tables, and while this was going on, the guests drank sweet wine and ate sweets and fruit, such as quinces, jelly, gingerbread, marmalade, cinnamon sticks, spice-cakes or marzipan. Often this after-dinner course, which was known as a *banquet*, was served in the withdrawing chamber, but sometimes family and guests retired to a special room.

These special places were often in exotic locations: a turret on the roof (Source 1), in the garden (Source 2), even on an island in the lake. The Tudors loved these fancies - and fashionable hosts loved to provide them.

Banqueting Houses

Source 2. Banqueting House in the gardens at Montacute House in Somerset.

Ideas
- Ask pupils to design their own banqueting house in the school grounds. What should it look like?

Religion

The dramatic religious changes carried out by the Tudors were bound to have an impact on important families and their houses. In 1534 Henry VIII declared himself Head of the Church in England. In 1536 smaller monasteries were dissolved and over the next three years all the others surrendered to the King's Commissioners.

Before the Dissolution there were over 600 religious houses in England and Wales. All their lands, property and possessions now passed to the Crown. If this wealth had stayed in royal hands over the next century our history might have been very different, with a rich monarchy independent of parliamentary taxes. However, Henry VIII's expensive wars in the 1540s led him to sell off most of the monastic property. The buyers were pleased with their new assets and therefore had a vested interest in the Protestant Reformation. While some people bought former monastic land, woods, fields and farms, others bought the monastic buildings themselves. Most were pulled down, but some were converted to dwellings. At Buckland Abbey in Devon (Source 4), Sir Richard Grenville actually converted the abbey church itself into his house. The same thing happened at Mottisfont Abbey in Hampshire. At Anglesey Abbey in Cambridgeshire, the old chapter house was converted into living accommodation, and at Lacock Abbey in Wiltshire the upper parts of the cloisters were turned into a house.

Roman Catholic Recusants

Roman Catholics were put in a difficult position by the events of the later sixteenth century. In most cases their wish was to worship in their own way, while remaining loyal subjects of Queen Elizabeth. This became increasingly difficult; Elizabeth was excommunicated in 1570 by the Pope, who absolved all Catholics from their obedience to her. A few were involved in plots to depose her. From 1574 Roman Catholic priests secretly came to this country to sustain English and Welsh Catholics, and hostility to Catholic Spain grew. This was all that the more militant Protestants needed to begin attacking Catholics. They were fined for not attending church; priests could be executed.

Several established families decided to stay loyal to their Roman Catholicism. In fact, it was the power and safety of these Catholic houses which kept Roman Catholicism alive in this country.

Coughton Court in Warwickshire was the home of the Throckmorton family, who had built the fine gatehouse seen in Source 3 in 1509. They took part in a plot in 1583 to murder Elizabeth and put Mary Queen of Scots on the throne. It was also at Coughton, in 1605, that the relatives of the Guy Fawkes plotters waited to hear if their scheme to assassinate James I had succeeded.

Several families made 'priest's holes', special hiding places to conceal priests from the government agents who were looking for them. These priest's holes survive at a number of Tudor country houses, including Speke Hall and Baddesley Clinton. Source 2 is an account of hiding in a priest's hole at Baddesley Clinton during a raid in the 1590s.

Source 1. Stained glass in the Chapel at The Vyne.

In Hiding

A Roman Catholic priest, John Gerard, describes hiding in the 'priest's hole' at Baddesley Clinton, Warwickshire, in the 1590s:

It was about five o'clock in the morning when I suddenly heard a great uproar outside the main door. It was the priest-hunters. There were four of them, with swords drawn and they were battering the door to force an entrance. Father Southwell heard the din, guessed what it was, slipped off his vestments and stripped the altar bare. While he was doing this, we laid hold of all our personal belongings: nothing was to be left to betray the presence of a priest. Our beds presented a problem as they were still warm. Some of us went off and put them cold side up to delude anyone who put his hand in to feel them. We then stowed ourselves and all our belongings into a very cleverly built sort of cave.

At last these leopards were let in. They tore madly through the whole house, searched everywhere, pried with candles into the darkest corners. They took four hours over the work but fortunately they chanced on nothing.

When they had gone, and gone a good way, so that there was no danger of their turning back suddenly as they sometimes do, a lady came and called us out of our den. The hiding place was below ground level; the floor was covered with water and I was standing with my feet in it all the time.

*Source 2. From **The Autobiography of an Elizabethan** by John Gerard.*

Ideas

- Did the family who owned the house your pupils are visiting benefit from monastic property? What did they buy? Did it help to change their fortunes?

- Is the house built on a former monastic site? What clues are there to tell us about this? Are there windows? Stonework? Cellars? Does the layout still follow the monastic plan, with buildings grouped round a cloister?

- In the religious strife of the sixteenth century, which side was taken by the family in the house at the time? Are there any clues in the house to suggest this?

- Are there priest's holes? How much room do they give a priest in hiding? How long do pupils think he could stay there?

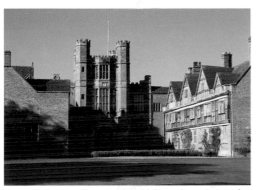

Source 3. Coughton Court in Warwickshire, where relatives of the Gunpowder Plotters waited to hear if the scheme had succeeded.

Source 4. Buckland Abbey was converted into a house after the Dissolution of the Monasteries.

33

Smaller Tudor houses

One of the successes of the Tudor monarchs was to make their court the centre of political and social life. If you wanted to be close to power, influence, excitement and spectacle, the court was where you had to be; skulking in your remote castle, surrounded by your liveried retainers, was no longer an option.

The career of Ralph Sadleir is an interesting case. His father got the contract to supply all the canvas for the Field of the Cloth of Gold, Henry VIII's extraordinary meeting with King Francis I of France in 1520. At about the age of fourteen, Ralph entered the household of Thomas Cromwell, then secretary to Wolsey but later to become the King's Chief Minister. By 1527 Ralph had risen to be Cromwell's secretary and by 1535 had made the important leap into royal service, working on the Dissolution of the Monasteries.

In 1533 Ralph built himself a brick house in Hackney (now called Sutton House, Source 3), the village where he was born. Hackney - only three miles from the City of London but still in the country - was a popular place for courtiers and merchants to live. Sadleir was knighted in 1540, served as Principal Secretary to Henry VIII and continued in royal service over four reigns. His last state appointment was as one of the judges of Mary Queen of Scots, in 1586. Sutton House, as his first house, proved too modest and he sold it in 1546, building himself a larger mansion near Ware in Hertfordshire.

Source 1. Trerice House, Cornwall, built in 1573 for Sir John Arundell.

The Gentry

The Tudor gentry were usually landowners of large but not enormous estates which they often farmed themselves. As food producers at a time of rising population and rising prices, they prospered during the sixteenth century.

Most gentry did not compete with the aristocracy in expensive pastimes like attendance at court or keeping a huge household, although they lived well, as Source 2 describes. They were the Justices of the Peace, Shakespeare's Shallow and Silence, on whom the Tudor government loaded all kinds of legislation. They wielded enormous power at a local level and often served as MPs; in the next century they were to challenge the monarchy itself.

Sources 1 and 4 show two of the many new gentry houses built in the sixteenth century.

Ideas

• The gentry were living more comfortably in Tudor times than ever before. Using the sources here and any smaller Tudor house that you visit, ask pupils to look for evidence of these improvements.

• What do pupils think of Henry Hastings' home (Source 2)? Would they like to live in it? Ask them to draw a picture, making use of their research into Tudor country houses.

Here and There a Polecat

The hall was strewn with marrow-bones, full of hawk's perches, hounds, spaniels and terriers. the upper sides of the hall hung with foxskins of this and the last year's skinning; here and there a polecat intermixed, guns and keeper's and huntsmen's poles in plenty. The parlour was a large room properly furnished; on a great hearth paved with brick lay some terriers and the choicest hounds and spaniels; two of the great chairs had litters of cats in them, which were not to be disturbed.

Source 2. Description of the house of Henry Hastings, a squire of Woodland in Dorset (1600).

Source 3. Sutton House, Hackney, was originally home of a wealthy Tudor courtier.

Source 4. Smallhythe Place, Kent - a 16th-century farmhouse.

Tudor Merchants

Peace and foreign trade brought prosperity to many people in Tudor England. Source 1 describes how contemporaries saw the rising standard of living affecting people well down the social scale. The historian W. G. Hoskins described the period 1540 to 1640 as 'the great rebuilding of England.' What he meant was that, wherever you go, farmhouses, townhouses and the houses of the great show signs of being improved or rebuilt in this period. As Source 1 explains, building a wall chimney was a common improvement, taking the smoke away from the centre of the room to give more pleasant living conditions. Putting in a ceiling, so that an old two-storey-high hall was turned into two rooms, one on each floor, was also common.

Trade

England had changed from being an exporter of wool to being an exporter of cloth in the later Middle Ages. Two parts of the country in particular devoted themselves to this trade: East Anglia and the West Country.

East Anglia - or to be more precise, north Essex and south Suffolk - was well-placed to trade with the Low Countries and had expertise in cloth-making. The houses, churches and guildhalls of Lavenham and Hadleigh in Suffolk testify to the wealth of the clothiers who ran this business - men who did not carry out any of the processes of spinning or weaving or fulling cloth themselves but had it all done by outworkers who were paid piecework. At Coggeshall, Essex, in the main street of the town is Paycocke's, a fine timber-framed merchant's house completed in 1505 (Source 3). The Paycockes were wealthy clothiers; the prosperity of the family can be seen in their tombs in Coggeshall church as well as in the elaborate decoration on the timbers. The house combines comfortable living quarters with business premises. Situated right on the street, one of its bays is given over to a wagon entrance so that loads of wool, yarn or finished cloth could be brought through to storage rooms or workshops at the back.

The West Country, and especially north Somerset and south Gloucestershire, was famed for broadcloths, which were exported to Antwerp. Several successful families in the area made the transition from trade to landowning. One such was the Hortons. Thomas Horton, a clothier and miller from Frome in Somerset, bought an existing property at Westwood Manor, near Bradford on Avon. Sometime before 1530 he improved and built on to the house (Source 4). The dining room and the bedroom above it, with their large windows, are his work. His punning *rebus* or badge, HOR over a barrel or *tun*, can still be seen in the bedroom window.

Rising Standards of Living

There are old men yet dwelling in the village where I live which have noted three things to be marvellously altered in England within their memory: the multitude of chimneys lately erected; the great improvement of beds, for we used to lie on straw sacks or rough mats, covered only with a sheet and a good round log under our heads instead of a pillow; and the exchange of vessels of wood into pewter, and wooden spoons into silver or tin.

Source 1. From **The Description of England**, by *William Harrison (1577)*.

Source 2. The Merchant's House, Tenby, Dyfed.

Source 3. Decorative carving on a doorway at Paycocke's, Coggeshall in Essex – a sign of the prosperity of the wool merchant who built the house.

Source 4. Westwood Manor was the home of a wealthy clothier, Thomas Horton.

The Great Elizabethan Houses

Right at the end of the Tudor period some extraordinarily spectacular country houses were built. Two of the most remarkable to survive are Montacute House in Somerset and Hardwick Hall, Derbyshire (Sources 1 & 2). Though very different, they illustrate similar ideas:

• They have symmetrical exteriors.

• They do not look into a courtyard but out at the world, the passer-by and the visitor.

• They are actually rather smaller than the great courtyard houses of the early Tudor period. By the end of the reign of Elizabeth households were shrinking. Having masses of retainers was not the way to impress: having a spectacular house was. (Bess of Hardwick's household was about fifty.) Montacute House looks enormous, but was in fact only one room thick in the centre block.

• They both express in visual form the Tudor belief in order and rank in nature and society (Source 3).

Montacute House was built by Edward Phelips in the 1590s. The Phelips were a gentry family who did well out of the Dissolution of the Monasteries. Edward then prospered at the law, became an MP and Speaker of the House of Commons in 1604.

Hardwick New Hall was built between 1591 and 1597 by Elizabeth, Countess of Shrewsbury, better known as Bess of Hardwick. Born in about 1520 at Hardwick Old Hall, a few hundred yards away, she was the daughter of a modest Derbyshire gentry family. She married four times, each time becoming richer and more prestigious.

Source 1. The entrance façade of Montacute House - looking out at the world rather than in on itself.

Source 2. Hardwick Hall - balanced and symmetrical.

Order and Rank are Natural and God-given

From the highest angel down to the lowest, every angel has a superior and an inferior. So from humans down to the meanest worm there is no creature which is not in some respect superior to one creature and inferior to another. So that there is nothing which is not included in this order.

*Source 3. Sir John Fortescue, **The Governaunce of England** (c.1473).*

Ideas

• Ask pupils to compare the pictures of Montacute and Hardwick. What similarities and differences are there?

• In what ways are they similar to the other houses of the Tudor period mentioned in this chapter? In what ways are they different?

• What Renaissance features are included in these two houses?

Hardwick Hall, Derbyshire

Hardwick Hall was built between 1591 and 1597 for Elizabeth, Countess of Shrewsbury. Notice her 'ES' monogram in stone on the parapet of the house.

Ideas

• The ground floor of Hardwick contains the Great Hall and many of the servants' work-rooms: the kitchens, buttery, pantry and scullery. The first floor contains the family's own apartments, and the second floor the state rooms. How does the house show this progression on the outside?

• Ask pupils to find the Great Hall. What is its size and importance now?

• Can they follow the route from the hall up to the High Great Chamber? How is it made to look impressive?

High Gr

Pearl Bedchamber

Best Bedchamber

Withdrawing Chamber

Long Gallery

Hall

Staircase

Investigating Portraits

As we piece together the lives of the people who lived in country houses in the past, it seems to help a lot if we can put faces to them. In the days before the photograph and the camcorder the nearest equivalent was the portrait.

But a portrait is not the same as the informal 'snap' or video that we rely on nowadays. It was painted over several sittings, with a much more calculated intention. Apart from royalty and the very famous, people probably only had their picture painted once in a lifetime, if at all. Obviously the artist can flatter the sitter: the ugly can be made beautiful by the skill of the artist's brush. But what else would they want the image to show? What would you want your portrait to say about you if it was the only picture of you in the world?

In the sixteenth and early seventeenth centuries, portraits often showed the sitter in an official capacity: wearing robes of office, or carrying some item specific to their job, like the white wand of the Official Controller of the Royal Household. Portraits might also include symbols - flowers or badges or jewels, for example - which told tell the viewer more about the life and personality of the subject.

In the great age of portrait-painting, the later seventeenth and eighteenth centuries, such formal signs and symbols were dropped; but even so, instead of asking, 'What did this person look like?', we would do better to ask 'What impression did this person want to give of himself or herself?'

The same applies even more strongly to royal portraits. In the sixteenth century it was a mark of loyalty to have a collection of royal portraits. Queen Elizabeth was fully aware of the importance of her image. Only approved pictures of her were allowed.

Pug, with Dunham Massey Hall, Cheshire, in the background (c.1700). Why was this picture painted?
What is the artist trying to tell us about the dog? About the house? What do you like about the picture? What do you dislike about it?

These were issued as sheets with tiny dots pricked in them as the exact, approved, outline. An artist would lay this template over a blank canvas and rub it with charcoal, giving the shapes which could now be painted in.

Examples of portraits can be found in almost all country houses. But three of the National Trust's properties contain special collections from the National Portrait Gallery: Montacute House, which contains pictures from the Tudor and Stuart periods; Gawthorpe Hall, Lancashire, which also has Stuart paintings; and Beningbrough Hall in Yorkshire, where there are portraits from the eighteenth century.

Thinking About Portraits

Here are some general suggestions to use with your class about when looking at portraits. There are also some questions under the three portraits on these pages.

- Take time to look at the image. What is your first impression?
- How much of the sitter do we see?
- What is s/he doing? What is s/he wearing? Is s/he holding anything?
- What is in the background?
- How do these features build up our impression of this person?

John Parker of Saltram, Devon, by Joshua Reynolds (1769). What is John Parker thinking? How would you describe him? What sort of man is he?

Elizabeth I, English School (c.1592).
Here are two pen-portraits of Elizabeth from different times in her reign:

Her hair was inclined to pale yellow, her forehead large and fair, her eyes lively and sweet but short-sighted, her nose somewhat rising in the middle, her lips narrow and her teeth black.
Sir John Hayward (1559).

Her face oval, fair but wrinkled, her eyes small but black and pleasant, her nose a little hooked, her lips narrow and her teeth black.
Paul Hentzner (1598).

How do these descriptions compare with her portrait? Which do you find more useful, the portrait or the written descriptions? Explain your answer.

**Chapter 3
The Stuarts
1603-1714**

**Learning
about the
Seventeenth
Century**

Children - and adults - can find it difficult to get to grips with the twists and turns of events in the Stuart years, 1603-1714. If we look at the history of some country houses we can make more sense of it all by seeing how family fortunes were affected by national events. Who stuck to their principles and who didn't? Who were the winners and losers at the end of it all?

Sometimes a house or castle played a key role in the military events of the Civil War. Look at Sources 1 and 2, for example. Sir John Bankes was Chief Justice to King Charles I and bought Corfe Castle in Dorset in 1635. When the Civil War broke out, as a Royalist he stayed in attendance on the King at his court at Oxford. His castle was besieged by Parliamentary forces twice, in 1643 and again in 1646. On each occasion his wife, Lady Bankes, organised the defence of Corfe. When it was finally captured, the Parliamentary forces blew up large parts of the ramparts - the ruins still stick out at crazy angles. During the Commonwealth the Bankes family were abroad in some financial hardship, but on the Restoration in 1660 Ralph, son of Sir John and Lady Bankes, was knighted. Corfe was damaged beyond repair, so Ralph settled at Kingston Lacy, also in Dorset, and built a new house there.

The Whitgreaves of Moseley Old Hall near Wolverhampton were prepared to put themselves in great danger for their King, as Source 5 describes.

Siding with Parliament was not necessarily a way of avoiding trouble. Thomas Myddelton of Chirk Castle in Clwyd (Source 3 and 4) organised the Parliamentary forces in North Wales. Chirk was taken by Royalist forces in 1642 and only retaken in 1646. The events of the 1650s caused Thomas Myddelton to declare himself for the King - rather prematurely, since Chirk was besieged, captured and partially destroyed in 1659. His family spent the next twenty years restoring it.

Powis Castle near Welshpool, a few miles away from Chirk, was owned by a Roman Catholic family, the Herberts. Myddelton captured Powis in 1644 and the Herberts did not live there again until 1660. Anti-Catholic hysteria led to William Herbert, Lord Powis, being imprisoned in the Tower from 1678 to 1683. He was one of the Catholic peers who James II brought into the government in 1685, to the scorn and amazement of many who considered themselves loyal monarchists. He went into exile with James in 1688.

A similar ruin nearly befell the Catholic Norris family, of Speke Hall. Sir William, who took over the house in 1606, made no secret of his religion. Fines for recusancy - refusing to attend Church of England services - and then the loss of their estates during the Civil War brought the family low. In 1651 Thomas Norris became an Anglican and revived the family fortunes.

The Hobarts of Blickling in Norfolk managed to steer a more successful course. Sir Henry Hobart was Lord Chief Justice under James I. His grandson took Parliament's side in the Civil War, married a daughter of John Hampden and sat in Cromwell's Upper House. However the Hobarts, like many families, were reconciled at the Restoration. Another Sir Henry Hobart was an enthusiastic supporter of the Glorious Revolution and fought with William III against James II at the Battle of the Boyne in 1690.

Source 1. A bronze at Kingstin Lacy in Dorset showing Corfe Castle under siege during the Civil War.

Source 3. Chirk Castle - besieged, captured and partially destroyed in 1659.

Source 2. After Corfe was captured, Parliamentary forces damaged it so that it could not be defended again.

Source 4. Thomas Myddelton of Chirk, organiser of the Parliamentary troops in North Wales.

This Gentleman Under Disguise

Charles II arrived at Thomas Whitgreave's house, Moseley Old Hall , after his defeat at the Battle of Worcester in September 1651. He was disguised as a woodcutter and accompanied by one of his courtiers, Lord Wilmot. Here is part of Whitgreave's account of what happened:

His lordship [Lord Wilmot] said to me, this gentleman under disguise is both your master, mine and the master of us all; and so, kneeling down, he gave me his hand to kiss.

...The next word after was where is that private place my lord tells me of? Which being already prepared and showed him, he went into it and when came forth, said it was the best place he was ever in.

Charles hid at Moseley while Parliamentarian soldiers searched the area, then escaped to France. After the Restoration, Whitgreave received a pension of £200 a year from the King.

Source 5.

Ideas

- If pupils studied a castle as part of *Medieval Realms*, what happened to it in the seventeenth century? How useful do they think early medieval castles like Corfe were in an age of gunpowder?

- If pupils are studying a particular Stuart house, they might investigate which side the family was on during the Civil War. Was this consistent from 1642 to 1660? Did they win or lose by this stand?

- What stand did the family take in 1688-9? Did they win or lose by this stand?

Jacobean Houses

The upheavals that took place during the reign of the Stuarts were matched by equally important changes in country house design. At the beginning of the seventeenth century the style was set by the palaces of the great courtiers who served James I. The huge amounts of money that courtiers made from their royal connections were lavished on their houses. For example, Hatfield House in Hertfordshire, built for Robert Cecil, Earl of Salisbury, and Audley End in Essex, built for Thomas Howard, Earl of Suffolk, were both intended to provide elaborate accommodation for royal visits.

Blickling Hall (Source 1) was built for Sir Henry Hobart, James I's Chief Justice, between 1619 and 1625. It was laid out by Robert Lyminge, who had designed Hatfield House, and has several of the same features: corner towers with lead cupolas, curving gables and a frontispiece in the middle of the main façade, with classical columns. Like late Elizabethan country houses such as Hardwick and Montacute, it was symmetrical on the outside, but not on the inside. The main rooms required were still a great hall, a great chamber, a parlour and a long gallery, and these rooms were now more heavily decorated (Source 2).

The architectural historian's task of giving a date to a style is sometimes made harder by the conservatism of builders. Sudbury Hall in Derbyshire (Source 3) was begun in the 1660s: yet the design of the exterior is really Jacobean, with its elaborate frontispiece and mullioned windows. The owner was George Vernon, who acted as his own architect. His building accounts have survived, telling us, for example, that one Thomas Phillips was paid 16s (80p) on 20 October 1668 for '16 big stones for cullomes'. Two years later Vernon paid £35 to carver and master-mason William Wilson 'to finish mee ye two frontispiece of my house, on ye top of ye front and backe porch as draughts'. The interior includes a long gallery, which was rather an old-fashioned idea by the 1670s, but Vernon was probably basing his plans for his new house on other mansions in the area, many of which had been built in Tudor times.

Now look at the picture of Felbrigg Hall, Norfolk (Source 4). The south front (right) was built in the 1620s by Robert Lyminge, who was working less than ten miles away at Blickling at the same time. The west front (left), built only sixty years later, obviously belongs to a completely different age.

Source 1. Blickling Hall, Norfolk - corner towers and curving gables.

Source 2. Detail of the ceiling in the Cartoon Gallery at Knole.

Source 3. Sudbury Hall in Derbyshire wasn't begun until the 1660s, yet the design of the exterior is basically Jacobean.

Source 4. Felbrigg Hall, Norfolk — two different styles and two different periods.

Ideas

- Compare Blickling Hall with Hardwick Hall (pp38-41). What had remained the same from Elizabethan to Jacobean times, and what had changed?

- Compare Sudbury Hall with Blickling Hall. What Jacobean features does Sudbury Hall have?

- In a Jacobean house, look for plasterwork ceilings and carved staircases. Which rooms are given the most elaborate treatment? What does this tell us about their importance?

- During a visit to a Jacobean house, ask pupils to try to match up the rooms on the inside with the symmetrical design of the outside. Has this produced any problems for the architect - blind windows, for example, or different floor levels disguised behind the mullions of windows?

The Formal Plan

The Civil War, the Commonwealth, and especially the execution of Charles I in 1649, changed England for ever. Although the monarchy was restored with great enthusiasm in 1660, in 1688 and again in 1714 the rightful monarch was denied the crown in favour of someone more acceptable to the real rulers of Britain, the wealthy landowners and merchants.

This change was reflected in dramatic alterations in the way country houses were built and lived in. During the Commonwealth many Royalists went to live in France and Holland. They were deeply influenced by European ideas of formality and ceremony; and some, such as the gentleman-architect Sir Roger Pratt, translated these ideas into homes for friends and acquaintances when they finally returned to England.

These new houses made important breaks with the past:

• Most of them were nothing like as big as the monster houses of courtiers. The gentry in particular had smaller households and wanted a more compact design. The 'double-pile', a type of house that was two rooms thick, met their needs: chambers were convenient, well-lit, well-heated and, because corridors allowed access without having to walk through someone's bedroom, much more privacy.

• The double-pile could also be made symmetrical inside as well as out, as you can see in the cutaway picture of Belton House on pp50-51. The most important rooms were in the centre, marked by a pediment (Source 3). Even the gardens focused on the centre of the house (Source 2).

• The later Stuart house was often raised on a basement. This made it look grander, and provided space for kitchens, storerooms and workrooms beneath the main body of the house.

• The hall became a grand waiting room for visitors (Source 1). It was furnished with chairs and impressive emblems of the family's importance.

• Other important rooms still included the great chamber - often called the saloon, after the French word salon - which was used for really grand occasions. Some houses now had a great parlour, used for formal dinner parties, and a little parlour, where the family normally ate. Both had their own withdrawing rooms.

• Apart from the kitchens, storerooms and workrooms in the basement and the servants' bedrooms, which were in the attics, the rest of the house contained suites of rooms, called apartments after the French word *appartement*.

Source 1. The Marble Hall at Petworth, Sussex - a grand waiting room.

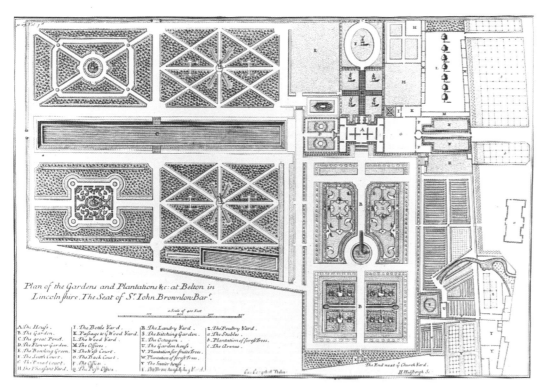

Plan of the Gardens and Plantations &c: at Belton in
Lincolnshire. The Seat of Sr Iohn BrownlowBart.

Source 2. The grounds of Belton House, Lincolnshire, in the early 18th century - geometry and formality.

Ideas

• Ask pupils to look at Source 2. How many lines converge on the centre of the house? How does the owner show his control over the gardens and the park?

• What geometrical shapes have been used in the design of Belton and its gardens?

• The plan of Belton is like an aerial view. But there were no aeroplanes or balloons at that time. How do pupils think the artist made the plan? (By making a measured survey of the site on the ground and then transferring it to paper.)

Source 3. Completed in 1701, Hanbury Hall, Hereford & Worcester, is a good example of a later Stuart house.

Belton House, Lincolnshire

Belton House was designed for the Brownlow family by William Winde, and built between 1685 and 1688. The wing on the left was for the family; that on the right contained grand apartments.

Bedchamber

Bedchamber

Withdrawing

Little Parlour

Marble Hall

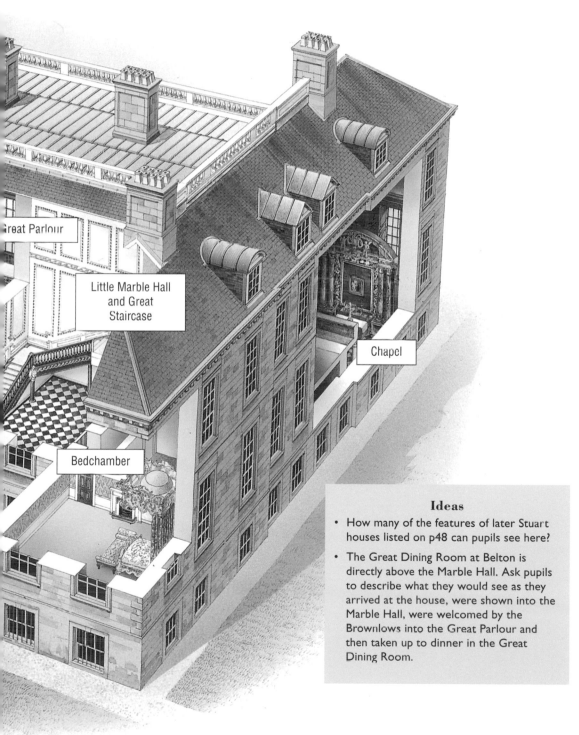

Great Parlour

Little Marble Hall
and Great
Staircase

Chapel

Bedchamber

Ideas
- How many of the features of later Stuart houses listed on p48 can pupils see here?
- The Great Dining Room at Belton is directly above the Marble Hall. Ask pupils to describe what they would see as they arrived at the house, were shown into the Marble Hall, were welcomed by the Brownlows into the Great Parlour and then taken up to dinner in the Great Dining Room.

Visiting

The later seventeenth century was an age of absolutist monarchs, and the kings and queens of Europe took their cue from the greatest of them all - Louis XIV, King of France from 1643 to 1715.

Louis built up an image of himself as the focus of all power: to be near him was to be close to the centre of influence. His every move was a ritual which emphasised this - even when he got dressed in the morning, he did so more or less in public, with great significance attached to who was present in the room, who was in the next room, who was two rooms away. The layout of Louis' great palace at Versailles made this clear, with suites of rooms in sequence, leading to the great state bedchamber. Britain, of course, had resisted absolutist monarchism - that was what the Glorious Revolution of 1688 was all about. But this did not mean that hierarchy had no place. In the Middle Ages and for some time afterwards, your power was measured by the number of people around you; but by the later seventeenth century it was measured by how exclusive you were. Houses were built with apartments of two, three or four rooms (Source 3). At the core - as at Versailles - was the bedchamber. Leading out of this were one or more ante-chambers, waiting rooms and withdrawing rooms. And beyond the bedchamber was the most intimate room of all: the closet, a small, richly decorated and personal room (Source 4). It was sometimes called after its French equivalent, the *cabinet*. The King's Cabinet Council of advisers met in his private cabinet, which is how the word came to be used for the closest advisers of the Crown.

When you visited someone, your status was indicated by how far the owner came through the rooms to greet you, how far you were invited through the sequence of rooms, how long you stayed and what you sat on. All this can be seen in Source 2, a description of a visit by the King of Spain to Petworth House, Sussex. Note that the King only went to the door of his bedchamber to meet the Prince, but he - and the Duchess in her turn - went right outside their apartment to greet the King. However, the Prince was welcomed right into the King's Bedchamber, and given an armchair to sit on - one up from an armless chair and two up from a stool.

Source 1. The south front of Ham House, Surrey.

A Royal Visit

The King of Spain visited Petworth House in Sussex in 1703. The Duke of Somerset had put Petworth at the disposal of Prince George of Denmark, husband of Queen Anne. When the King arrived, George showed him to his apartment:

[He] there left him about half an hour, after which he sent to visit him, and was received at the door of his bedchamber by His Catholic Majesty and seated in an armchair opposite to his own. The ceremony was short and the Prince had not been long retired to his quarters before the King sent to return the visit and was received at the top of the stairs and conducted to the Prince's bedchamber.

The King then asked to meet the Duchess, who 'came forward several rooms, even to the bottom of the stairs to meet the King.'

Source 2. From **Annals of the Reign of Queen Anne** (1704).

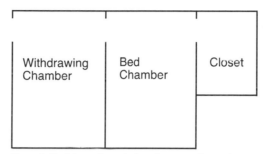

Source 3. *Good, better, best - the formal sequence of rooms in an apartment.*

Source 4. *A closet like this one at Ham House was small, richly decorated and very personal.*

Ideas

- Look for a state apartment in a late seventeenth- or early eighteenth-century country house. How many rooms does the apartment contain? What are they? Is there a progression of greater luxury as you approach the bedchamber? How is it clear that the bedchamber was used for entertaining as well as sleeping?

- Ask pupils to imagine that they are visiting someone in this apartment. As they approach, they can probably see right through to the far end. The doors are all in line. Why do pupils think the architect lined up the rooms so that you could see right along them in this way?

- Play the game of Formal Visiting:

  Player A visits Player B. Player B throws the dice to see where Player A is met: 1 or 2 - outside the apartment; 3 or 4 - in the Antechamber; 5 or 6 - in the Bedchamber.

  Player A throws the dice to see where they sit down: 1 or 2 - in the Antechamber; 3 or 4 - in the Bedchamber; 5 or 6 - in the Cabinet.

  Player B throws the dice to see what A will be invited to sit on: 1 or 2 - a stool; 3 or 4 - a chair without arms; 5 or 6 - an armchair.

  Player B then visits Player A. Who ends up with higher status?

Servants

The way wealthy people wanted to live in the late seventeenth century meant a change in the position of the servants in the house. The huge medieval household, which had continued into Tudor and even early Stuart times, finally disappeared. In 1620 at Knole - admittedly a very large house - there were 111 servants; by the end of the century, Chirk Castle had forty-five servants and Belton House only twenty-five.

One reason for this was that status no longer depended on how many retainers you had. Law and order were well-established and a standing army removed the need for leading people to retain their own private armies.

Owners of country houses now wanted to lead polite, fastidious lives. Even senior servants were no longer companions and near-equals; they just had to do their work as unobtrusively as possible. Sir Roger Pratt ruled that 'The house should be so contrived that the ordinary servants may never publicly appear in passing to and fro.' Although some servants still spent time in the hall, waiting to be sent on errands, they now ate in their own servants' hall in the basement. Nor did owners want to meet their servants on the main staircase. Backstairs were built, so that the domestic staff could reach all parts of the house while remaining out of sight of family and guests.

In this situation the status of servants fell. No longer were the upper servants the offspring of gentry, learning about society and building up connections. The law, trade, the armed forces and the colonies provided better openings. Unlike his medieval forerunner, the steward now looked after the house only, with a land steward in his own separate house employed to manage the estate. In the past the steward had been a leading member of the household, with up to three servants of his own. By the early eighteenth century, at £80 a year he was below the master of music and the head gardener, on £100 each.

Female Servants

Many more women were employed as servants as the seventeenth century wore on, partly because they were cheaper. The Duke of Chandos' great palace in Middlesex, Cannons, had not only laundry-maids and dairymaids (two of the few jobs in the medieval household often done by women) but also three housemaids, two cookmaids and a charwoman. The duties of some of these servants are described in Sources 2 and 4.

The most senior female position was that of housekeeper. At around £10 a year she was paid much less than most of the men, but she ate at the same table as the upper male servants and was in charge of the 'dry' larder - tea, coffee, sugar, preserves and other groceries.

Source 1. A 17th-century servant.

Wash and Smooth the Linen

Pray inquire for a chambermaid for us & that you may fully acquaint her with our business I have sent you an account of what it is that we expect from her. She must make & mend for him & me & for my son & sister, she must wash & smooth all the fine linens & muslins & dress our heads & keep our chambers neat & clean. The Dairymaid, when her cows are milked, the poultry & swine fed, shall help her wash that part of the house that is not in constant use; but our lodging chambers that we lie in every night, she must do them by herself.

Source 2. From a letter from Lady Judith Danby of Swinton Hall, Yorkshire (c.1704).

Source 3. A reconstruction of the Stuart kitchen at Ham House.

Ideas

- Ask pupils to read through Sources 2 and 4, looking up any words they do not know. What did these two servants do? Is one job better than the other?

- When would pupils rather have been a servant - in medieval times, in a large mostly male household? Or in an smaller household of the early eighteenth century, when more women were employed, and when most worked in the basement and slept in the attics? What reasons can they give for their choice?

- Divide the class into pairs. Give them the information on these pages and read them p6, about the medieval household. One person in the pair is a medieval servant, the other is employed in an early eighteenth-century household. They should discuss their jobs, their relationship with their employer, and their living and working conditions.

Keep Your Kitchen Clean

Wash your kitchen every night, and the larders every other day... and scour the pewter we use every Friday night, and all the rest of the pewter once a month. Keep your kitchen extraordinarily clean. Help the rest of the maids to wash on washing days. Make all the maids bring down their candlesticks first thing in the morning to be made clean.

Source 4. From the household regulations at Bank Hall, Liverpool (1677).

Dining in Stuart Times

At Belton House in Lincolnshire there were three rooms where meals could be taken. The largest, for most formal and important occasions, was the Great Dining Room, in the most important place in the house: the centre of the front, on the first floor. Here Sir John Brownlow entertained King William III in 1695. Twelve fat oxen and sixty sheep were killed for the feast and 'the King was exceeding merry and drank freely.'

For slightly less grand dinners the Brownlows used the Great Parlour. Everyday meals were taken in the Little Parlour.

None of these rooms held anything like as many diners as a medieval great hall. The important factor now was not the quantity of guests, but their quality. Similarly, the luxury of the furniture and fittings of the rooms, and the stairs which led to them, reached new heights. At Belton the Great Dining Room was panelled, the Great and Little Parlours had tapestries on the walls. At Ham House (Source 3) the hangings were of gilded leather, which did not absorb the smell of food. Ceilings were plastered in much more refined designs; compare Source 1 opposite with Source 2 on page p47 from earlier in the century.

For a formal meal the room was set rather like a restaurant is today, with high backed armless chairs at several tables - often gate-leg tables which could be folded when not in use. All these can be seen in Source 3. Rooms were lit with candles or rushlights, often set in sconces whose polished silver backs reflected their light.

Tables were laid with knives and spoons, as formerly, but forks were increasingly provided after 1660. This meant that napkins were not so necessary and they became merely decorative (Source 2). Pewter, widely used from the late sixteenth century, was difficult to clean, and retained scratch marks. Although wooden plates continued to be used by servants, the wealthy began to use glazed pottery or 'Delftware'. English-made glasses began to replace metal, clay and wooden cups from the 1670s.

The elaborate medieval ritual for serving meals described on pp10-11 finally disappeared. The food offered up followed much the same pattern as in Elizabethan times, with two courses made up of many different dishes. These were arranged on the table in careful symmetrical designs. The third course, of sweets and fruits, was now called, in the French way, a *dessert*.

Ideas

- Ask pupils to make a list of all the ways in which a formal dinner party in late Stuart times was more refined than a similar occasion a hundred years earlier.

- Here is the first course for a meal held by the 4th Earl of Dorset at Knole in 1636:

  Rice pottage

  Barley broth

  Buttered young pike

  Scrambled eggs

  Boiled cow's udders

  Roast tongues

  Bream

  Perches

  Roast veal

  Mutton stew with anchovies

  Pike

  Fish pasties

  Roast venison

  Two capons

  Three wild duck

  A whole salmon

Cut out a large oval piece of paper for the table, and smaller round or oval shapes for the plates. Write on each plate the name of a dish from the menu above. Pupils can lay the table in an attractive and symmetrical pattern.

Source 1. Stuart decoration in the Dining Room at Dunster Castle, Somerset.

Source 3. Ham House - hangings of gilded leather did not absorb the smell of food.

Libraries and Closets

The attitude towards learning expressed in Source 2 was quite typical among the upper classes in the sixteenth century. They were no longer expected to make war as their favourite hobby, but a brave and dashing performance on the hunting field had simply replaced the expectation of a brave and dashing performance on the battlefield.

There were exceptions, of course. Humphrey, Duke of Gloucester, had a good collection of books in the fifteenth century; and Tudor monarchs were among the best educated rulers of Europe in their day. Nevertheless, 92 out of 146 Northumberland gentry in the 1560s could not sign their own name. The inventory of Hardwick Hall reveals that Bess - who was certainly an educated woman - owned only six books.

By the Stuart era things were changing. More and more country house owners were literate, and increasingly interested in collecting books. The first libraries begin to be built into houses after 1660. In 1713 James Gibbs began work on the Library at Wimpole Hall in Cambridgeshire to house Lord Harley's vast collection of 50,000 books and 350,000 pamphlets (Source 1).

Collecting

The passion for collecting went further than books, however. Many followed the lead of Charles I and began to collect works of art. Wealthy British collectors began to travel, buying paintings and sculpture all over Europe.

In the seventeenth century there was increasing interest in all kinds of knowledge, but very little specialisation. The Royal Society, established in the early 1660s with Charles II as its patron, had eminent scientists among its members, but also many interested amateurs, not least the King himself. Collectors, or virtuosi as they were called, brought together all kinds of objects: fossils, archaeological finds, crystals, historical relics, globes, clocks, botanical and biological specimens. Some of these collections were of genuine scientific or historical interest. Others were just curiosities.

Where was it all to go? Some houses had galleries which could house these objects. In others, the closet, the owner's most private little room, provided the setting for these personal collections. The Green Closet at Ham House is only 20ft by 16ft, yet in 1670 it contained 55 paintings.

Source 1. The Library at Wimpole Hall, built in the 18th century to house Lord Harley's vast collection of books and pamphlets.

Source 2. The Green Closet at Ham House – an intimate setting for its owner's collection of precious objects.

Down With School

I'd rather that my son should hang than study letters. For it becomes the sons of gentlemen to blow the horn nicely, to hunt skilfully and elegantly, to carry and train a hawk. But the study of letters should be left to the sons of rustics.

Source 3. A gentleman's view of education (early 16th century).

Ideas

- In the closet (sometimes called the cabinet):

  How big is this room? What evidence has it got of the personal taste of the owner(s) of the house? What does the room and its contents tell us about them?

- As your pupils go round a country house, ask them to look out for evidence of collecting.

Investigating Plans

Many guidebooks to country houses contain plans. These are obviously important for finding your way about, but using a plan prior to a visit can often be the best way for pupils to 'discover' the building before they actually see it.

• Plans allow pupils to take in the whole house at once. This may well not be possible when they are there - it may appear a jumble of buildings, or have at least two quite different façades, dating from different periods. It may hide internal features behind a later façade.

• Plans give a sense of the overall pattern of a house. Look at Castle Coole in Co. Fermanagh built at the end of the eighteenth century. The plan shows clearly how the rooms fit round the Hall, the pairing of Dining Room and Drawing Room, how the Bow Room above uses part of the curve of the Saloon below, why the stairs are where they are and so on. Combined with a picture of the outside, we can tell how the house 'works' as a whole, before looking at the individual rooms when we get there.

• At Castle Coole we can take this investigation of the overall idea of the house even further, by using the plan to measure the sizes of the rooms. The four rooms at the four corners of the main block are the same size, all using a 6ft module, 36ft by 24ft. They are also 18ft high. Carrying out comparative measurements on the plan is far easier than doing it on site, even if this was allowed.

Thinking About Plans

• Is the house symmetrical or asymmetrical in plan?

• Space is the main commodity at the architect's disposal. What are the largest spaces? What were they used for? What are the smallest spaces? What were they used for? Are the small spaces for unimportant people? Or for greater comfort and intimacy?

• How would you get around the house? Did the architect want people to take certain routes? Would you take a different route if you were one of the servants or a guest of honour?

• What route would a visitor take from the main entrance to the most private room of the host or hostess?

• What route would the food take from the kitchen to the dining room?

• What route would people take from the room where they were being entertained to their bedroom at the end of the evening?

• Who would pupils expect to find in each room? When would they expect to see them there? (They might add drawings of these people, in costume, to an enlarged photocopy of the plan of the house they are studying.)

• Are there certain rooms which were used mainly by men or mainly by women? If both, how do they relate to each other?

• Compare a plan with a picture of the house. Can pupils tell which side of the house the picture shows? Does the outside hide what is going on inside? Or does it tell them something about the rooms inside - perhaps by emphasising one or two of them? If the outside hides the plan of the inside, does this present any problems - having windows in the wrong place, for example?

Castle Coole, Co. Fermanagh, built at the end of the 18th century.

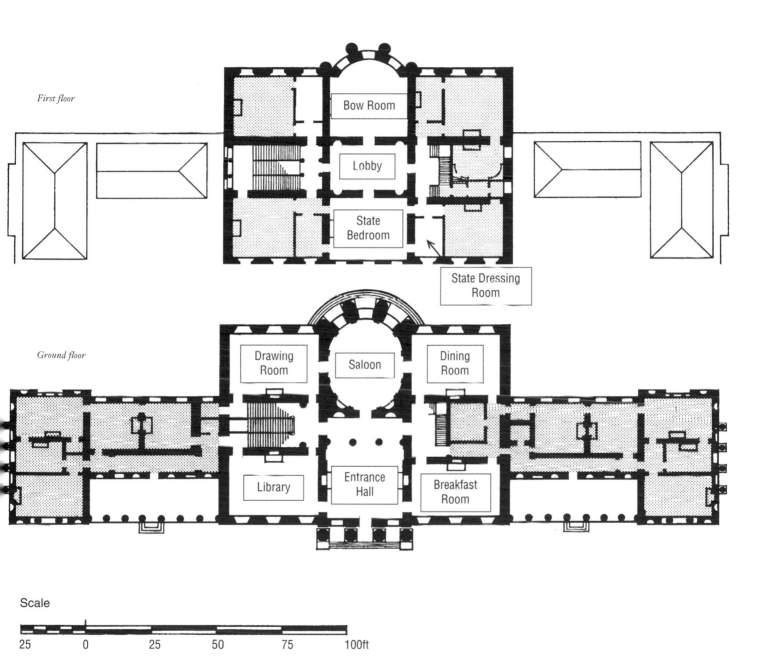

First floor

Bow Room

Lobby

State Bedroom

State Dressing Room

Ground floor

Drawing Room

Saloon

Dining Room

Library

Entrance Hall

Breakfast Room

Scale

25   0   25   50   75   100ft

A modern guidebook plan of Castle Coole showing the areas now open to the public. What are the largest spaces? What are the smallest spaces? How would Georgian visitors have moved through the house?

Life in Georgian Britain

In the Georgian period, perhaps more than any other, country houses were houses of power.

Before the Industrial Revolution, land was the main source of wealth and country houses were the centres of huge agricultural empires. Sir Nathaniel Curzon, the builder of Kedleston Hall in Derbyshire, owned 10,000 acres, and there were others with even larger estates. And as they came to realise that agricultural improvements could make their farms yield greater profits, landowners grew more and more interested in making those improvements. At Wimpole Hall in Cambridgeshire, for example, the 3rd Earl of Hardwicke built a new farm and introduced better drainage, new machines, crops and livestock (Source 2).

Increased wealth from agricultural improvement meant that Georgian landowners could spend plenty of money on their houses. Some were enormous, and many were decorated and furnished to a greater degree of luxury than had ever been seen before.

Political Power

After the upheavals of the seventeenth century, Britain was still a monarchy - but monarchs had little real power. That now lay with Parliament, and with the great landowners who controlled Parliament by gaining the support of the relatively small number of people who could vote.

Gone were the days when great lords were judged by the sheer numbers of hangers-on who flocked round them. Some estates still gave the occasional feast, but it was often held outside or in the servants' hall. This change can be seen in the two quotations in Source 4.

Social Power

While barriers grew between those who owned property and were therefore entitled to vote, and those who did not, relations within the property-owning classes were becoming more relaxed. At Bath, Beau Nash welcomed anyone to his assemblies,

Source 1. The family relaxing in the grounds of Belton House in the 18th century.

provided they knew how to behave properly. A new type of less formal socialising came to replace the stiff ritualised behaviour of the seventeenth century (Source 1). People mingled, talked, danced, played cards or ate together. In towns, this might happen in assembly rooms. But in the country, great houses were the usual setting, and the double-pile Stuart house, with its formal apartments in straight lines, was not really suitable.

What was needed was at least three large rooms opening out of each other, so that crowds of guests could circulate freely. These were usually grouped round a central, top-lit hall (Source 3). Perhaps the most important room was the saloon, grandly

decorated and with its furniture set against the walls to allow as much space as possible for 'meeting polite persons of both sexes for the sake of conversation, gallantry, news and play'. At Kedleston Hall (pp68-69) there are two circuits of grand rooms round each side of a central hall and saloon.

Source 2. Georgian farm buildings at Wimpole Hall.

Source 3. The 18th-century Hall at Mount Stewart House, Co. Down.

Ideas

- Look back over the previous chapter: were Stuart houses suitable for the kind of large-scale socialising described here? If pupils owned such a house, how would they go about making it usable for the kind of grand balls and assemblies the Georgians were expected to hold?

- Show pupils a room plan of a Georgian house such as Castle Coole (p61). How do the rooms open out of each other to provide good opportunities for circulating?

- How would pupils organise a Georgian house they know for a grand ball for 200 people? Where would they have the dancing, the card-playing, the eating? Where would people sit to talk?

Idle Loose Fellows

In 1720 the Duke of Chandos ordered that all visitors to his house:

> **if honest substantial men, and not idle loose fellows, be asked to drink before they go away and more especially this be observed towards tenants.**

In 1735 the Duke of Newcastle stopped the practice of:

> **giving small beer and doles of wheat to all the people of the country about them and of entertaining all comers and goers, with their servants and horses.**

Source 4.

The Classical Legacy

Eighteenth-century aristocrats were tremendous admirers of ancient Greece and Rome. Many of them completed their education by going on a Grand Tour of Italy, looking at classical sites (Source 1). The Roman architect they most admired was Vitruvius, whose ideas had been taken up by an Italian, Andrea Palladio, in the sixteenth century. Palladian ideas were slow to catch on in Britain, partly because they were favoured by Charles I and his architect, Inigo Jones, and so were seen as the architecture of Royalism. But after 1714, when the Stuart monarchs were rejected a second time, the Palladian style was adopted by the great landowners who had invited the Hanoverians to take the throne.

Stourhead House in Wiltshire (Source 2), designed by Colen Campbell in 1720 for a banker, Henry Hoare, was based on one of Palladio's villas. The Palladian style made use of classical features such as columns and pediments, as Source 2 shows, and involved exact mathematical measurements to achieve what the Georgians believed were perfect proportions. The Hall at Stourhead, for example, is an exact cube. The height of the Hall at Clandon Park, a Palladian house in Surrey, is exactly half its length and one-and-a-half times its width.

At Kedleston Hall the architect Robert Adam based his design for the south front on the Arch of Constantine in Rome. The Entrance Hall at Kedleston is like an *atrium*, the central courtyard of a Roman house. The marble pattern on the floor imitates the fountain and pool that would have stood there.

Classical motifs, like the Osterley panel in Source 3, were used to decorate the interiors of Georgian houses.

Source 1. Many wealthy Georgians completed their education with a Grand Tour of Europe.

Empires

Why all this admiration for the classical world? The Romans felt they were superior to all other peoples. They considered their rule brought benefits to the people they conquered (Source 4). In the eighteenth century, the British ruling classes were building an empire in America, India and the Caribbean. They too felt that they had a right to rule and a duty to rule well. At Kedleston there are panels with classical scenes in the entrance hall, but in the saloon the panels show great events from British history. The message seems to be that the British are the heirs of the Roman tradition.

Spare the Humble

Remember, Roman,
To rule the people under the law, to establish
The way of peace, to battle down the proud,
To spare the humble. These are, forever, our fine arts.

Source 4. Virgil (1st century BC).

Source 2. Classical features at Stourhead House, Wiltshire (1720-25).

Ideas

- Outside a Georgian house:

  Look out for classical features, such as columns, capitals, pediments, balustrades.

  Look for strong horizontal lines in the design. What about the proportions of width to height, over the whole front, and over parts of the building such as the portico?

- Inside a Georgian house:

  Look for classical features, as on the exterior.

  Look also for people and stories from Greece and Rome, in statues, carved panels, pictures, tapestries.

  Ask pupils to try to estimate whether the dimensions of the rooms follow mathematical rules.

Source 3. Classical decoration at Osterley Park, Middlesex.

Orderly Landscapes

Georgian landowners wanted to show that their power extended not only throughout their country house, but into the garden and beyond to the whole landscape visible from the windows of house. The effect they wanted to create was that the house stood in an ideal setting, part ancient Rome, part historic England. All that should be seen was order and beauty. During the eighteenth century, for example, the grounds at Stowe in Buckinghamshire were laid out with temples and monuments. Most were classical in design but were given English purposes. There is a Temple of Concord which celebrates English victories at the end of the Seven Years' War in 1763. There are monuments to Captain Cook and General Wolfe. There is a Temple of British Worthies containing fifteen busts of heroes from King Alfred to John Locke - and one heroine, Elizabeth I. There is a Temple of Ancient Virtue, celebrating Roman qualities, and there used to be a Temple of Modern Virtue. This was built in ruins, to show disapproval of the Prime Minister, Robert Walpole. The Gothic Temple (Source 3) is a deliberate exception to the classical theme. It celebrates what were seen as ancient English liberties: Magna Carta, trial by jury, an elected Parliament.

By the middle of the eighteenth century more attention was being paid to the overall setting of these classical features in the landscape. At Stourhead (Source 2) the stream in the valley below the house was dammed in 1765 to produce a lake. As well as skilful planting of exotic and native trees and shrubs, the landscape setting included classical temples, a grotto, even the medieval market cross from Bristol - all contributing to a series of carefully contrived views across the lake. Guests staying at the house could walk around this lake, or ride past it up to a monument to King Alfred erected in 1762 on the hill above.

Many landowners brought in professional landscape designers to remodel the setting of their houses, men such as Lancelot 'Capability' Brown and

Source 1. These 'before' and 'after' views of the landscape at Wimpole Hall show how Humphry Repton demonstrated his ideas to clients.

Source 2. Stourhead – classical features in the landscape.

Humphry Repton. Brown started as gardener at Stowe in 1741 and went on to work on a huge scale all over the country. Repton began work in 1788 and used his own water-colours to make 'before and after' overlays to demonstrate to his clients the changes he would carry out (Source 1).

Ideas

- The class can make its own Georgian landscape. Take a photo of a country scene, or find one in a magazine, and use it as the basis for a mural. Ask pupils to draw and cut out temples, arches, ruins, grottos, statues and obelisks, and place them in the 'landscape' to make a picturesque view.

- Create your own Repton 'before and after' views. Take a photo of an ordinary piece of landscape nearby, perhaps your school playing field. Discuss with the class how they would make it more interesting to look at. They might want to add a lake, clumps of trees, a view. They can paint their ideas on pieces of paper and stick them onto the original.

Source 3. The Gothic Temple at Stowe celebrates ancient English liberties.

Kedleston Hall, Derbyshire

Kedleston Hall was built for Nathaniel Curzon, 1st Baron Scarsdale. It was begun in 1758, but the project was taken over by Robert Adam in 1760.

Saloon

Dressing Ro

Library

Hall

Drawing Room

Music Room

Family Corridor

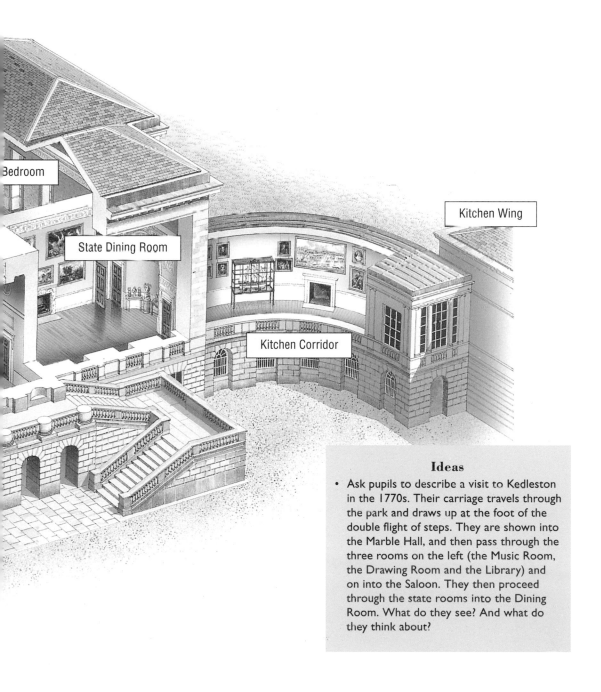

Bedroom

State Dining Room

Kitchen Wing

Kitchen Corridor

Ideas

- Ask pupils to describe a visit to Kedleston in the 1770s. Their carriage travels through the park and draws up at the foot of the double flight of steps. They are shown into the Marble Hall, and then pass through the three rooms on the left (the Music Room, the Drawing Room and the Library) and on into the Saloon. They then proceed through the state rooms into the Dining Room. What do they see? And what do they think about?

Georgian Interiors

Besides giving balls, the Georgian country house owner entertained guests at formal dinner parties. These started at about three o'clock in the afternoon, and often did not end until ten at night. Guests met in the saloon or drawing room. When dinner was announced they would process into the dining room in strict social order. Women sat at one end of the table and men at the other. The meal lasted two or three hours. After the dessert course, the women would leave the table and go into the drawing room for tea, while the men stayed on drinking.

This distinction between a mainly male dining room and a mainly female drawing room is often reflected in the decoration. At Attingham Park, Shropshire, there are two paired suites of rooms, with dining room, library and Lord Berwick's study on one side and two drawing rooms and a boudoir for Lady Berwick on the other.

Apartments of Conversation

[Dining rooms are] apartments of conversation, in which we are to pass a great deal of our time. This renders it desirable to have them fitted up with elegance and splendour, but in a style different from that of other apartments. Instead of being hung with damask, tapestry etc. they are always finished with stucco and adorned with statues and paintings, that they may not retain the smell of the victuals.

Source 1. Robert Adam (1773).

Robert Adam

The architect Robert Adam (1728-92) designed not only the structural elements of a house, but also the decoration of walls and ceilings, the carpets and furniture. He even stipulated how pictures should be arranged on the walls. Adam was well-informed about classical architecture, having spent several years in Italy studying Roman buildings at first hand.

His ideas for dining rooms can be read in Source 1 and seen in action in Source 2. Source 3 shows a drawing room decorated by Adam. The delicacy and refinement of his designs are shown in Source 4.

Rather wilder decoration can be seen at Claydon House, Buckinghamshire (Source 5).

Ideas

- In a mixed school, pupils could discuss what makes rooms male and female in character. Then ask them to design their own living rooms, down to the last detail of carpets, wall-coverings, pictures, furniture and fittings. Are the designs of the boys different from those of the girls? If so, in what ways?

- Show Source 4 to your pupils. Ask them to cut pieces of paper to fit the inside of a shoe box. They can add a door in each end wall, three windows in one long wall and a fireplace in the other. Then they should decorate the walls in Adam's Etruscan style.

Source 2. Adam's design for the buffet in the Dining Room at Kedleston Hall.

Source 3. Osterley Park - an Adam drawing room.

Source 4. The Etruscan Room at Osterley shows the delicacy and detail of Robert Adam's interiors.

Source 5. Rococo decoration - a Chinese tea party at Claydon House, Buckinghamshire.

The Sublime

For some, the restrained straight lines of Palladian buildings lacked drama. They missed what the eighteenth-century writer Edmund Burke called 'the Sublime'. According to Burke, 'a rotund form, in presenting no checks to the eye, simulates infinity'.

A number of round or oval houses were built during the Georgian period. The present Claydon House in Buckinghamshire, for example, was originally one of a pair of buildings joined by a huge rotunda; put up in the 1760s and 1770s, the rotunda had been demolished by the end of the century.

Perhaps the grandest of all 'round' houses is Ickworth in Suffolk, built between 1795 and 1829 (Source 1). Ickworth's owner was Frederick Hervey, known as the 'Earl-Bishop' because he was both 4th Earl of Bristol and Bishop of Derry (Source 2). Hervey was enormously rich, with an income of £40,000 a year, and keen on round buildings - he had already built a round house on his estate at Ballyscullion, Co. Donegal, and a temple in the form of a rotunda at Downhill, Co. Londonderry. His idea was to use the great central rotunda at Ickworth for living and entertaining and to fill the two side wings with his enormous collection of works of art and antiquities. He saw it as a combination of the British Museum and the National Gallery.

Unfortunately the Earl-Bishop died before the house was complete. His son thought of demolishing the half-finished structure but decided to turn the east wing into a family home, using the central rotunda for entertaining and showing works of art.

Party Time

By the end of the eighteenth century, country house life-styles had changed. Better transport on improved turnpike roads meant that guests could come for visits of just a weekend or a few days. It was the beginning of the age of the country house-party. Source 3 describes its informality. A mixture of ages and sexes met for serious political business, or for match-making, or just to enjoy themselves.

Houses were no longer raised up on a basement floor. There was a wish to be closer to nature, so that rooms opened straight on to lawns, and were filled with pots of flowers. Conservatories, orangeries and colonnades (Source 4) were built, creating rooms

Source 1. Ickworth in Suffolk - 'a rotund form, in presenting no checks to the eye, simulates infinity'.

Source 2. Frederick Hervey built a number of round houses, including Ickworth.

which were halfway between indoors and the grounds outside. With no raised basement, servants' quarters were either underground or in separate wings, from which the staff could be summoned by a system of bells and bell-pulls.

Ideas

- What does the class think about round and oval houses? Would they like to live in one? Would it be fun?

- What problems are involved in building and furnishing a round house? How would pupils divide up the interior to create rooms? What would they do about carpets and large pieces of furniture? Would outside doors and windows have to be curved as well?

Play Till Suppertime

The house was crowded - a thousand comers and goers. We breakfasted between ten and eleven, though it is called half past nine. We have an immense table - chocolate -honey - hot bread - cold bread - brown bread - white bread - and all coloured breads and cakes. After breakfast the Duke's chaplain, Mr Scott, reads a few short prayers, and then we go as we like - a back room for reading, a billiard room, a print room, a drawing room, and whole suites of rooms, not forgetting the music room... There are all sorts of amusements; the gentlemen are out hunting and shooting all morning. We dine at half past four or five - go to tea, so to cards about nine, ...play till suppertime - 'tis pretty late by the time we go to bed.

Source 3. An account of an Irish house party (1779).

Source 4. Wimple Hall, Cambridgeshire - conservatories like this formed halfway houses between indoor rooms and the gardens outside.

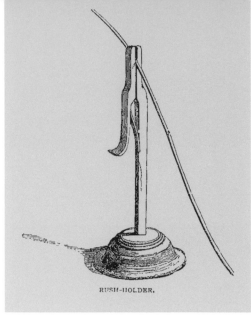

RUSH-HOLDER.

A rushlight holder. Rushlights were cheap, but smelly.

One of the themes of this book is the continuing search by house-owners for ways to make their homes more comfortable. In practice, 'more comfortable' often meant 'warmer and lighter'.

In our climate, living in a country house must have involved being quite cold through the winter months. The best one could hope for was to create islands of warmth in a generally chilly atmosphere. In medieval, Tudor and early Stuart times, curtains, hangings and tapestries cut out the worst of the draughts from windows and doors. The four-poster, with its four, five or six curtains making a small draught-free zone, meant at least it was possible to stay warm in bed.

Fires and Fireplaces

The open fire in the middle of the early medieval great hall, kept permanently alight, must have been a welcome source of heat, although at the price of lots of smoke and draughts. The lord's solar was at least a little more comfortable. It usually had a sunny aspect and either a fireplace of its own or a portable brazier.

Wall fireplaces were gradually introduced during the Middle Ages. A number of devices were used to make the most of the heat from the fire. To

A wall sconce at Knole.

burn well, logs have to be propped up at one end. This was achieved by *andirons* or firedogs. From the sixteenth century onwards, thick cast-iron firebacks, often with a coat of arms or scene cast into them, picked up the heat and radiated it out. Sometimes the heat was so fierce that small wicker or wooden screens were provided to prevent women from acquiring a flushed face, regarded as unbecoming.

Coal fires became more common from the eighteenth century. They needed much smaller fireplaces and just a small, raised grate. For large spaces cast-iron stoves were also used. But the fireside was such a symbol of home that even in Victorian times enormous chimneypieces were still the norm. At Cragside in Northumberland a vast inglenook was installed in the 1880s. It burned turf (peat) and modern technology was only used to carry away the smoke in a concealed flue to a hidden chimney in a pile of rocks on the hillside.

Light

Before the invention of electricity most people lived their lives by daylight, rising and retiring more or less with the sun. This explains the fact that in the Middle Ages, for example, mealtimes were much earlier than they are today, especially in winter.

But rooms were still lit, of course. Rushlights were made by gathering rushes in late summer, when they were fully grown but still green. The thin ends were cut off and the green skin peeled away, leaving one strip to support the soft pith. The rushlight was allowed to dry and then dipped eight or nine times in melted fat (usually mutton-fat) and allowed to set between each dipping. It was then held in a special holder at an angle, burning for fifteen or twenty minutes - and producing a rather nasty fatty smell.

Beeswax candles, though much more expensive, were longer lasting and gave a much stronger light. By the seventeenth century various devices were used

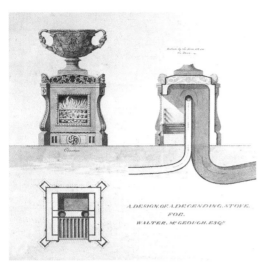

Design for a stove at The Argory, Co. Armagh.

This vase at Cragside was converted into an electric light in 1880.

Crystal chandelier in the State Drawing Room at Kedleston Hall.

to make the best of available light. Candles were often set on 'sconces', plates of silver or other polished metal fixed to the wall behind the candle to reflect its light. For big occasions chandeliers for dozens of candles would be hung from the ceiling. However, much of a country house would be unlit after dark and there were many portable candle-holders to light one's way around.

In Victorian times, colza oil and (especially after the development of the incandescent mantle in the 1880s) gas were both popular forms of lighting. But towards the end of the century electricity made its appearance. Cragside, home of the inventor and engineer William Armstrong, was one of the first houses in the world to have its own electric light. Light bulbs perfected by Armstrong's friend, Joseph Swan, were fitted in the vases in the Library at Cragside in 1880.

Thinking about Heating and Lighting

Pupils can use the table on this page to explore the heating and lighting needs of a country house.

Name of room	Heating needs (low/high)	How is it heated?	Lighting needs (none/low/high)	How is it lit?

Old and New in Country Houses

What can country houses tell us about Victorian times? After all, at this time Britain was the most industrialised country in the world. Land was no longer the main source of wealth and power. With the 1832 Reform Act, eighty-six 'rotten' or 'pocket' boroughs, usually controlled by landowners, lost one or both of their MPs, twenty-one large towns gained two MPs and seventeen more towns gained one MP. In 1846 Parliament decided that cheap food for factory workers was more important than protecting British farmers, and repealed the Corn Laws. By 1851 a majority of Britain's population was living in towns or cities.

Yet the country house way of life remained as appealing as ever (Source 2). Old families stayed in their ancestral homes, sometimes diversifying into industry by exploiting mineral resources on their estates, or investing in business. New families with new money bought or built themselves country houses, like John Heathcoat Amory, who owned a textile factory in Tiverton and built Knightshayes

Court in Devon; or Theodore Mander, a paint manufacturer of Wolverhampton, who built Wightwick Manor on the outskirts of the city; or William Armstrong, the inventor, engineer and arms manufacturer, who created a huge estate at Cragside.

And what sort of country houses did they want, these wealthy Victorians? With money and new technology they could take their pick from the world's materials and architectural styles, past and present. If you wanted Elizabethan, you could fill your house with 'Tudor' interiors, as the Lucy family did at Charlecote Park in Warwickshire (Source 1), or add Jacobean details to a Georgian house, as Disraeli did with Hughenden Manor, Buckinghamshire. At Penrhyn Castle in Gwynedd the Pennants, with money from Jamaican plantations and Welsh slate quarries, made an enormous 'Norman' castle (Source 3), with ducted warm air central heating, hot and cold running water and flush toilets. Parts of Cragside (pp78-9) are half-timbered, a style of building almost unknown in

Source 1. Elizabethtan Revival decoration in the Dining Room at Charlecote Park, Warwickshire.

Northumberland. Its Library (Source 4) has an Italian Renaissance ceiling, with Japanese decoration, oriental vases, Goanese chairs and Egyptian onyx round the fireplace.

Ideas

- Use the guidebook to the Victorian house your class is visiting to find out how the builders made their money. Is there any evidence at the house to show the source of their wealth?

- Which period has provided the inspiration for the architectural style of the house?

- How has the architect managed to combine Victorian convenience and comfort (bathrooms, electric light, central heating radiators, running water) with the historic style of the house?

Log Fires, Comfort and Warmth

It was a very big house, grey, and spreading itself about, with a gallery stretching from one end of it to the other - a place of ample fireplaces and log fires, comfort and warmth, the browns and reds of leather chairs, and dark pictures in gilt frames, with a piano at one end and an untidy pile of music on the ottoman beside it.

Source 2. Constance Sitwell recalls country house life in the 1890s.

Source 3. The Neo-Norman Hall at Penrhyn Castle, Gwynedd.

Source 4. A cosmopolitan interior - the Library at Cragside .

Cragside

A small Victorian villa at Cragside was remodelled and considerably enlarged between 1869 and 1884 for the Newcastle inventor and armaments manufacturer William Armstrong. His architect was Richard Norman Shaw. The house blends several architectural styles; there are medieval crenellations, Tudor chimneys, Gothic arches. It also includes a number of Armstrong's technological improvements - hydraulic lifts, hydro-electric power and electric light.

Ideas

- On the exterior of the house, ask pupils to find and identify different architectural styles.

- What do the pupils think of the combination and the impression that it gives? Do they like the look of Cragside, or not? And why?

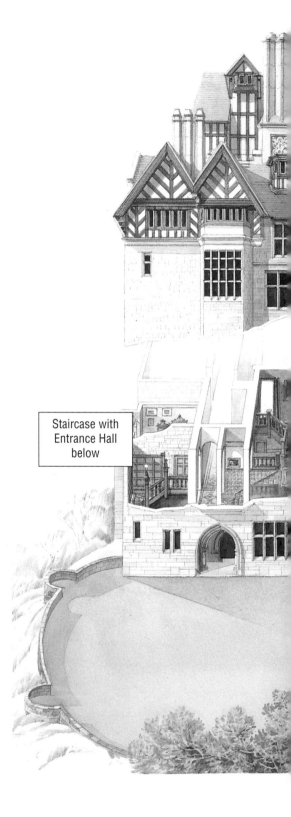

Staircase with Entrance Hall below

Watercolour Gallery

Tower Room

Drawing Room

Gun Room

Gallery

Billiard Room

The Victorian Family Home

Lord Byron may not have been a typical Georgian, but Source 1 represents all that horrified the Victorians about their predecessors - moral irresponsibility, hard drinking and irreverence. And in reacting to what they saw as Georgian decadence, Victorian country house owners wanted to give the impression of a quiet, sober, family home.

There are relatively few signs in earlier country houses of the presence of children, who were usually fostered out to wet nurses when they were babies, and treated as pets or miniature adults when they returned. But in the nineteenth century children's rooms were placed near their parents and care and attention was given to nurseries (Source 2).

Philanthropy

Wealthy Victorians didn't only take an interest in their children; many of them also looked after the welfare of their tenants and the surrounding villages. For example, the Trevelyans of Wallington in Northumberland built new cottages for their estate workers; the Manders put up a village hall and a home for retired governesses at Wightwick, and the Aclands of Killerton in Devon built cottages and village schools.

Country house owners often spent great sums in building or rebuilding local churches (Source 3); and, after falling out of fashion in the eighteenth century, house prayers were once more taken seriously. Owners felt they should encourage a higher moral tone than their Georgian ancestors; the Trevelyans of Wallington, for example, were teetotal. Bachelors' and young ladies' bedrooms were placed in opposite wings of the house. The moral welfare of servants was also closely supervised (Source 5). As we shall see, servants' quarters were planned so that as little mixing of the sexes took place as possible.

Source 2. The late Victorian day nursery at Wightwick Manor, Wolverhampton.

Pistols in the Hall

Our average hour of rising was one. I generally got up between eleven and twelve and was esteemed a prodigy of early rising. Then for amusement there was reading, fencing or shuttlecock in the great room, practising with pistols in the hall, cricket, riding, sailing on the lake, playing with the bear or teasing the wolf. Between seven and eight we dined and our evening lasted from that time until one, two or three in the morning. I must not omit the custom of handing round, after dinner, a human skull filled with burgundy.

Source 1. A guest describes a house-party at Lord Byron's home, Newstead Abbey in Nottinghamshire (1809).

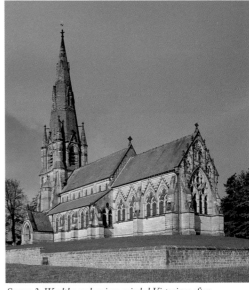

Source 3. Wealthy and serious-minded Victorians often spent huge sums on building new churches like this one, at Studley Royal in North Yorkshire.

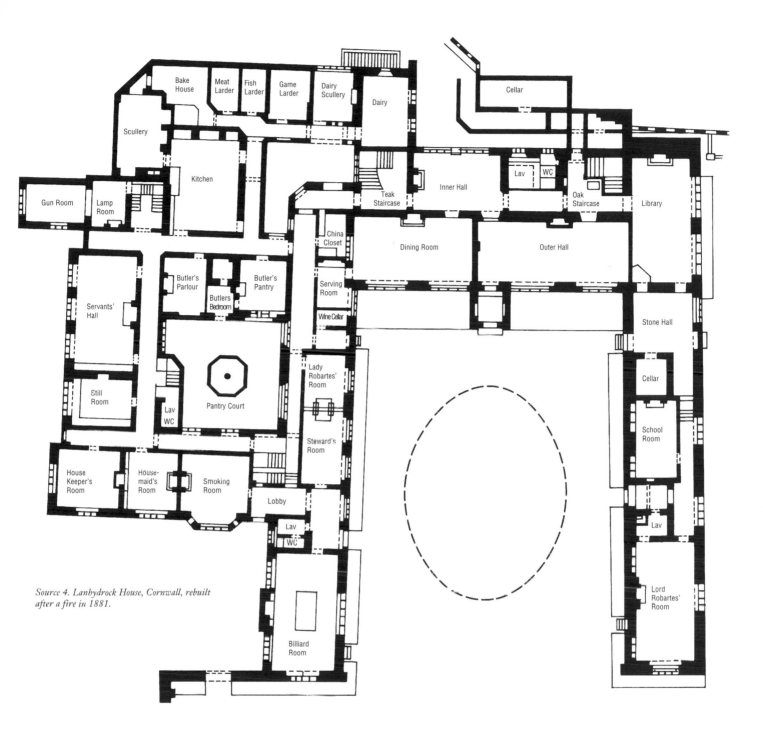

Source 4. Lanhydrock House, Cornwall, rebuilt after a fire in 1881.

Keeping the Servants in Order

At prayers he explained how he came to be in possession by God's blessing on his labour, that we were to remember not only to be a help to our poor neighbours but examples too and that as there would always be plenty in the house he wished never to see or hear any of his servants being seen or heard of in a public house - he did it kindly but very firmly.

Source 5. A new owner moves into Blackmoor House in Hampshire (1866).

Ideas

- Look at the house plan of a Victorian country house. Where did children sleep? Is it near their parents? Where was the nursery? Was there a schoolroom? Are there any other special children's rooms or buildings?

- Does the house plan show segregated bedroom areas?

- How do your pupils react to Source 5? Does it show a fatherly responsibility? Or a patronising interference in people's lives?

The Baronial Hall

In addition to good works in the locality, many Victorian country house owners wanted to live up to an ideal of medieval hospitality (Source 1). On big occasions, like Christmas and the coming of age of the eldest son, great dinners and dances were held. A large hall was needed, preferably with a sort of medieval look about it, to conjure up images of Merry England.

Architects had to make sure that new houses were not only comfortable and welcoming, but also grand and awe-inspiring. After all, their owners were important people who often entertained eminent guests. The hall therefore once again became one of the largest and grandest rooms in the house. Great beams and rafters were left visible, as in a medieval hall. At Knightshayes Court there are stone carvings of medieval people at work.

However, the Victorian great hall could not be a bare, draughty room with long tables and benches, like a real medieval hall. Instead, it was well-furnished with carpets, big armchairs and settees (Source 2).

The division of the other parts of the house into male and female areas continued. The drawing room remained an important female area (Source 3). The original decoration for the drawing room at Knightshayes, designed by the eccentric architect William Burges, featured a chimneypiece like a medieval castle, with women on the ramparts and knights laying siege below, on the theme of 'The Assault on the Castle of Love.' Sadly Burges' client, John Heathcoat Amory, didn't like the design and it was never carried out.

Under Oak Rafters

They did not confine their guests to a few fashionables, who condescended to pass away a few days occasionally in a country house; but under the oak rafters of their capacious halls the lords of the manor used to assemble all their friends and tenants at those successive periods when the church bids all her children rejoice.

Source 1. The architect Augustus Pugin describing what he thinks of the hospitality offered in medieval houses (1841).

The morning room was also a women's domain, and the library mainly male. But the most exclusive male preserves were the smoking room and billiard room, which usually adjoined each other (Source 4). Sometimes, as at Cragside, the gun room, another male zone, was nearby. Many houses banned smoking except in the smoking room, to which men would withdraw (women didn't smoke in mixed company until the end of the century), wearing special smoking jackets, to play billiards, drink, smoke cigars and engage in man-talk.

Source 2. The Great Parlour at Wightwick Manor - grand and awe-inspiring, or comfortable and welcoming?

Ideas

During a visit to a Victorian country house, ask pupils the following questions:

- Is the hall grand and awe-inspiring or comfortable and welcoming? Is it possible to be both? How like a medieval hall is it? Are there any aspects of the decoration which add a medieval feel to it?

- How far are the smoking and billiard rooms from the drawing room? Is there any evidence that these rooms were used exclusively by men?

- Look at the house-plan in the guidebook. How far is the division of rooms into male and female areas taken in the layout of the house? How far is this division taken in the decoration of the rooms?

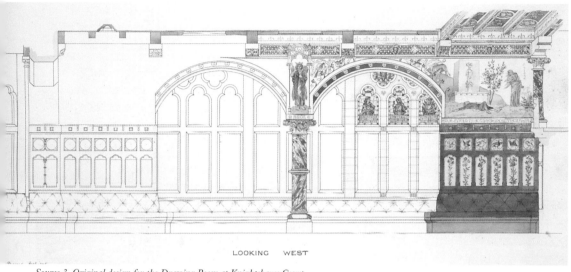

LOOKING WEST

Source 3. Original design for the Drawing Room at Knightshayes Court.

Source 4. The Billiard Room at Lanhydrock - a male preserve.

Dining in Victorian Times

By 1900 Queen Victoria ruled a quarter of the world, an empire on which the sun never set. These international links were reflected in country houses in many items of decoration and furniture as well as in the food the Victorians ate.

Foodstuffs from all over the world were available: exotic fruits, grain from Canada and, from 1880, frozen meat from Australia. Indian curries appeared on British menus. Recipes were more sophisticated, often prepared by French chefs who, with salaries of £120 per year, were the most highly paid servants. Victorian hothouse gardening put early vegetables and tropical fruits on to the menus of country house dining-tables (Source 4).

And wealthy Victorians ate an enormous amount of food. Breakfast was the most informal meal, at about 9am, with cold meats, pies, eggs and bacon, fish kedgeree, sausages, kidneys, rolls or toast and tea or coffee.

Lunch was a comparatively modern meal, although you could still be offered a joint and vegetables, followed by fruit. Women were beginning to hold lunch parties as an exclusively female form of entertaining.

Tea, at about 5pm, was a nineteenth-century innovation introduced to fill the lengthening gap between lunch and dinner. It would consist of sandwiches, cakes, muffins, scones, bread and butter, with jams and honey.

Dining

Dinner, at about 8.30 or even 9pm, was still the most formal meal. Guests would arrive and meet about a quarter of an hour beforehand. They would go into the dining room (Source 3) in pairs, with the host and the most important lady leading, while the other guests followed in order of importance.

Menus, in French, divided the food in the way we know today (Source 1). It was no longer the fashion to put all the dishes on the table at once; servants served them course by course. Tables were elaborately decorated, with a white damask cloth reaching down to the ground, white napkins, flowers in vases, fruit in dishes and a large centrepiece of china, glass or metal to hold flowers or candles. Each place-setting needed several knives, forks and spoons and up to three glasses for different kinds of wine.

Food was brought up from the kitchen and kept hot just outside the dining room door. At the end of the meal the women would rise first, leaving the men to talk and drink. At some houses chamberpots were discreetly provided (Source 2).

However, this male interval only lasted for about a quarter of an hour, in contrast to the long, drunken sessions of the Georgians. Then the host would ask, 'Shall we join the ladies?'

A Victorian Dinner Menu

FIRST COURSE

Mock turtle soup.

Brill and lobster sauce.

Fried whitings.

ENTREES

Fowl à la Béchamel.

Oyster patties.

SECOND COURSE

Roast sucking-pig.

Stewed rump of beef à la jardinière.

Vegetables.

THIRD COURSE

Grouse.

DESSERT

Charlotte aux Pommes.

Coffee cream. Sweet omelet.

Apricot Tart. Iced pudding

*Source 1. Mrs Beeton's **Book of Household Management** (1861).*

Source 2. Chamberpots were discreetly provided in some dining rooms.

Source 3. A late Victorian dining room - Standen, West Sussex.

Source 4. Victorian hothouse gardening put early vegetables and exotic fruits on many country house dining tables.

Ideas

- In the dining room of a Victorian house, ask pupils to look at the table arrangement and place-settings. What is each item for?

- How far is the dining room from the kitchens? What evidence is there of ways of keeping food warm, or re-heating it after its journey from the kitchens?

- What items would Victorians use to eat each dish from the menu in Source 1?

- Wealthy Victorians ate a lot. A doctor wrote, 'The stomach is the mainspring of our system; if it be not sufficiently wound up to warm the heart and support the circulation the whole business of life will, in proportion, be ineffectively performed.' What evidence of this attitude is there in the text and sources on these pages?

Cooking and Kitchens

The complicated meals shown in the menu on page 84 needed a large kitchen and lots of servants. The French chef at Cliveden in Buckinghamshire, for example, had five female assistants. Victorian kitchens were often huge (Source 2), to give plenty of room for all these people to work, and to prevent conditions from becoming too hot. The main items of furniture were usually a great table for preparing food, a couple of Windsor chairs to rest in occasionally, and the cooking range. This was made of cast-iron, one of the new products of Britain's industries. Ranges were sometimes open, but as the nineteenth century wore on, the closed range became more popular. In big houses, there were two: one at a low heat for simmering soups and stews, and another at a high heat for roasting and baking. The hot range could take four days to reach its proper temperature.

There was usually no oven thermometer and chefs had to know their ranges. One book suggested throwing a piece of white paper into the oven: if it burned the oven was too hot. If it turned dark brown the oven was ready to cook pastry. Light brown was right for pies, dark yellow for cakes and light yellow for puddings and biscuits.

The range had to be swept once a week, the ash emptied, the ovens cleaned inside and out, the iron black-leaded and any other parts polished. This job was usually carried out by the second kitchenmaid, who was paid around £14-£20 a year.

The Victorian age was a great age of gadgetry. There were new machines for chopping, grinding, mincing, slicing, peeling potatoes, stoning cherries, even shelling peas, as well as the new necessity, a tin-opener. The floors of work areas were scrubbed once a week and covered with fine sand. Walls were covered with another new industrial product: glazed tiles, which were easy to keep clean (Source 4).

By no means all the cooking was done in the kitchen. Most houses had a scullery, where vegetables were prepared and cooked and the washing-up done (Source 1). Scullery maids were the lowest of all servants, earning £12-£18 per year.

There were special larders for storing food - ideally a dry larder, a fish larder and a meat larder. In houses with large farms attached, there might also be a dairy. Special attention was given to the design of dairies to keep them cool and hygienic (Source 4). Cold water flowed over marble slabs and milk was kept in water-cooled tanks. Cheese, butter and cream were prepared here.

Source 1. The scullery at Lanhydrock, showing the slate sinks for washing up, the wooden drying racks and the small range for cooking vegetables and simmering stock.

Ideas

In a Victorian kitchen:

- Ask pupils to look out for the kitchen range. Does it tell them who made it? How did it work? Where was baking done? Roasting? Simmering? How would they cook a roast meal here?

- Is there any evidence that the nineteenth-century kitchen equipment has replaced earlier fittings?

- Look for the pestle and mortar, still the most common kitchen utensil. What other gadgets are there?

- Is there any evidence of factory-made articles, such as tin pastry-cutters, jelly and pie moulds, mincing machines, egg whisks, tin-openers or knife-cleaners?

- What items are exactly the same as the ones we use now and which do we no longer use at all? What is their modern equivalent?

- What would it be like to work here in summer? In winter?

- How would pupils set about preparing the food for the menu on p84? What ingredients would they need and how would they prepare them?

Source 2. Wallington, Northumberland - Victorian kitchens were often huge.

Source 3. The range in the Victorian kitchen at Speke Hall.

Source 4. The dairy at Lanhydrock.

The World of Work

The Victorian country house contained special areas for every task carried out by the servants. This led to the growth of a warren of little rooms, so that servants' quarters took up nearly as much space as the grand state rooms and family accommodation.

There were four departments of servants. We have already seen that the kitchen included scullery, larders, stores and a dairy. This was under the management of the *chef* or, in smaller country houses, a female 'professed cook.'

The *butler*, in his black dress coat and white bow tie, was the most imposing and the most senior male servant, in charge of all the footmen. In fact, by the end of the nineteenth century, he might be the only male servant. He was responsible for the serving of meals, the wines, and all the general management of the household, including its security. A host and hostess who entertained a lot valued the services of a skilled butler. The butler's pantry was the centre of his empire (Source 2). The board showing all the bells in the house was just outside. He had the keys to the cellar and the strongroom and slept nearby to keep an eye on it all.

The *housekeeper* was in charge of all the maids. She was responsible for keeping the house clean, and for the stores of tea, coffee, sugar and other groceries. She looked after the all the linen and ran the stillroom, where jams, cordials, cakes, biscuits and preserves were made (Source 3). Her room, business-like but cosy, was a popular gathering-place for the senior servants.

The fourth department was the laundry (Source 4). Here the *laundrymaids* filled copper tubs with water, which was heated. Shredded soap was added, then the clothes, tablecloths and other linen agitated by a dolly-peg. Wooden washboards were used for scrubbing. The clothes were then rinsed and drained in wooden sinks and put through the rollers of a wooden mangle. After drying - outside when possible - they were ironed with heavy flat-irons which were heated on a special stove, then aired. All this was hard work, but laundrymaids had more independence than most servants, as they were not under the direct supervision of anyone else.

Source 1. Estate worker - Edward Barnes, the woodman at Erddig in Clwyd in the 1830s.

Ideas

- Show pupils the plan of Lanhydrock on p81. How much space do the servants' quarters take up? How does this compare with a house from an earlier period?

- Can the class work out which rooms belonged to the chef or cook, the butler and the housekeeper? Which had control of the biggest proportion of the servants' area?

- Why do modern visitors often like the servants' quarters of a country house the best of all?

Source 2. The butler's pantry at Cragside.

These Charming Girls

These charming girls, in their thin muslin gowns and sandalled shoes, fluttering from garden to still-room, like bees depositing their loads of sweets...There still remain jars of pot-pourri and a few bottles of elderflower water over a hundred years old.

Source 3. The wife of the owner of Springhill, Co. Londonderry, remembering stillroom maids in her youth (1946).

Source 4. The dry laundry at Erddig.

Separate Worlds

Large Victorian country houses often employed between twenty and forty indoor servants (Source 1). Some of those at Dunham Massey, together with their wage rates, can be seen in Source 2. The number of servants, and the low wages for which they were prepared to work, were two of the reasons why modern technology was so slow to catch on at many country houses. It was more expensive to install central heating and running water in all the bedrooms than to pay servants to make up fires and carry jugs of hot water upstairs.

Wealthy Victorians felt that they were responsible for the morals of their servants. Men's and women's sleeping quarters were quite separate and workrooms were arranged so that male and female servants did not run across each other more than was absolutely necessary.

The Servants' Hall

Servants would start work about 6am, making sure that fires were going and hot water ready in the bedrooms before the family and guests got up. Breakfast was at 8am. The upper servants would eat in the housekeeper's room, while the others ate in the servants' hall (Source 4), which was usually placed between the male and female working areas and was one of the few places where men and women on the staff could meet. At 9am all the servants joined the family and guests for prayers.

Lunch was a snack eaten at about 11am, while dinner was a hot meal eaten by all the servants together in the servants' hall at 1pm. Tea was at 4.30 and supper at 8.30. Many servants were finishing work by 11pm, but scullerymaids could not go to bed until all the washing up had been done.

It was a hard life with strict rules (Source 3), but there were compensations. Although you had to work long hours and always be at someone else's beck and call, you had a roof over your head and good food to eat. Some masters and mistresses were unreasonable, others were kind and generous. Most fell somewhere in between.

Source 1. A Victorian housekeeper at Erddig.

Ideas

- Ask pupils to get into pairs, and to make a list of all that they would dislike about being a servant in a Victorian country house. Then they should make another list of things they would like about the life. They can compare lists with other pairs.

- In thinking about the lives of servants, pupils must bear the alternatives in mind. What else could a young boy or girl do in Victorian Britain, in a town or in the country? Would they prefer to be a factory girl or a scullerymaid, a farm labourer or a footman? Why?

- The attitude of the master and mistress of the house to the servants must have made all the difference. In what ways could they make the lives of servants pleasant or unpleasant?

Position	Name	When Engaged	Wages p.a.
Butler	Charles Hughes	6 March 1901	£70
Footman	Andrew Jones	30 July 1906	£26
Cook	Grace Bennett	5 June 1906	£42
Kitchenmaid	Annie Parfitt	27 April 1906	£15
Housemaid	Isabella Collins	4 March 1898	£29 4s
Promoted to Housekeeper (Mrs)		19 March 1903	£40
Under Housemaid	Edith Knight	3 September 1906	£23
Lady's Maid	Sarah Sams	25 March 1901	£30
		March 1906	£35
Governess	Miss Edith Griffiths	28 April 1904	£35
Schoolroom Maid	Ethel Upton	27 March 1906	£8
Under Housemaid	Louise Bramley	25 June 1907	£10
Head Housemaid	G. Green	25 June 1907	£30
Motor Driver	George Drinkwater	24 April 1907	per week £2
(motor car delivered 27 April 1907)		(plus a room but not board)	
First Footman	Clement Long	1 August 1907	£40
2nd Footman	Herbert Olney	9 July 1907	£24
Kitchenmaid	Eleanor Price	8 August 1907	£24
2nd Kitchenmaid	Alice Watson	1 August 1907	£26
Scullery Maid	Edith Hepburn	1 October 1907	£12
Gardener	William Mingay	21 May 1909	per week 25s
2nd Housemaid	Florence Burrows	16 January 1909	£24
3rd Housemaid	Lizzie Green	25 May 1908	£18
4th Housemaid	Alice Cushion	2 November 1908	£10
Hall Boy	W. Benham	28 November 1908	£10

Source 2. Servants' wages at Dunham Massey, Cheshire, in the early 20th century.

A Few Paces Behind

Always move quietly about the house; do not let your voice be heard by the family unless necessary. Never sing or whistle at your work where the family would be likely to hear you. When meeting any ladies or gentlemen about the house, stand back or move aside for them to pass. Should you be required to walk with a lady or gentleman, in order to carry a parcel or otherwise, always keep a few paces behind.

*Source 3. From **Rules for Manners of Servants in good Families** (1901).*

Source 4. The Servants' Hall at Erddig.

The Twentieth Century

The twentieth century brought sweeping changes to the country house. The trend towards a new kind of country house owner which began in Victorian times - people who came from business or industry - increased; and many such owners wanted a house in the country to provide the romantic and authentic aura of history, with accommodation for country pursuits. They did not expect to live off landownership. In fact, agricultural rents were low from the 1880s to the 1940s. Old landowning families were forced to sell up, or turned from agriculture to other sources of income.

New buyers wanted the reassurance of an ancient country seat - but not its inconvenience. There was a boom in large extensions to small historic houses. Those who did build anew went for quiet romance - old bricks, tiled roofs, leaded windows, limed oak beams and deep porches. And even those who wanted to make a show turned to the past for inspiration. Castle Drogo (Source 1), begun in 1910 on a defensible site high on the edges of Dartmoor, shows that castles still held their magic, even though they had been obsolete for 500 years.

Many late nineteenth- and early twentieth-century houses have rambling plans; they are deliberately made to look as if they have grown slowly over many centuries. Nevertheless, central heating, ample garaging, lots of bathrooms and electric light were always included. A vague feeling that these things were not quite right lingered on, though: garages, light bulbs, radiators, even wash-basins were often hidden away or disguised as something else.

The modern conveniences in twentieth-century houses were partly the result of a wish for more comfort (Source 2), and partly an answer to the servant problem. With factories offering better wages and more personal freedom, it became harder and harder to get servants. Vacuum cleaners, central heating, hot and cold running water on all floors, electric lights, cars instead of horse-drawn carriages, more efficient cookers, all reduced the number of servants required to run a large house. There was no need for a bake house, still room or brew house when vans from local shops delivered daily. Guests expected to serve themselves at breakfast and lunch, if not dinner. Servants were given more time off, better wages and accommodation. The life of a servant of this time comes through vividly in Source 3.

The slaughter of the Great War hit country house families as it hit every family in the land. The Robartes family of Lanhydrock lost their eldest son; Julius Drewe, the builder of Castle Drogo, lost his eldest son in Flanders in 1917 (Source 4).

Yet it was the Second World War which really spelled the end for country houses. Some, such as Cliveden in Buckinghamshire and Standen, West Sussex, were taken over as hospitals; evacuees were housed at Waddesden Manor in Buckinghamshire and Lacock Abbey in Wiltshire. The treasures of the National Gallery were hidden away at Penrhyn Castle.

After the war there were no building materials for repairs. There were fuel shortages. Few people were willing to become servants. The two wars had shaken the social order. Deference to one's 'social superiors' was no longer acceptable to many people.

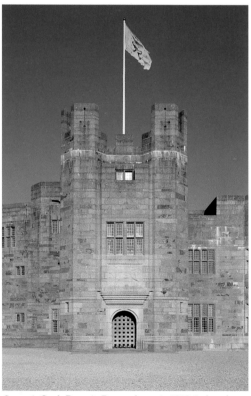

Source 1. Castle Drogo in Devon - begun in 1910, it shows how castles still retained their appeal even in the early 20th century.

Source 2. The Drawing Room at Castle Drogo - signs of a wish for more comfort.

Sooner or later death duties hit the country house owner's family, even if war and falling incomes had not already done so. Faced with high valuations of estates, antiques, paintings and chattels, but no great income, many families opted out. Country houses became corporate headquarters, schools, colleges, residential centres, golf clubs, Youth Hostels. And some, of course - more than 200, in fact - have come to the National Trust, to be cared for and protected for ever.

A Servant Remembers

I used to help the pantry boy wash up the silver; each item was washed separately in a wooden bowl and Heaven help you if the butler saw two items in the bowl at once. All the servants sat down to their meals very punctually. The butler sat at the head of the table in the Servants' Hall, with the housekeeper on his left. Footman and pantry boy were on his right and the cook at the other end. There would be about ten people for meals.

The food was first class. Breakfast always consisted of a huge amount of bacon and eggs. I would return for my dinner at 12 o'clock. This was a big roast: pork, lamb, beef etc. and home-grown vegetables. Tea consisted of a large variety of home-made cakes and bread.

Source 3. Reminiscences of a servant at Ormesby Hall, Cleveland, in the 1930s.

Source 4. Adrian Drewe, the son and heir of the builder of Castle Drogo, died in Flanders in 1917.

Resources

Further Reading

Aslet, Clive,
The Last Country Houses,
Yale (1982).

Bailey, B:
English Manor Houses,
Robert Hale (1983).

Beard, G:
The English House Interior,
Viking (1990).

Bisgrove, R:
The English Garden,
Viking (1990).

Carter, P G & Neal, P D:
'Historic houses and educational use:
some problems and solutions',
Head Teachers Review 69-3 (1978), 71-3.

Dalkeith, Earl of:
'Interpreting Bowhill',
Heritage Interpretation 35 (1987), 4.

Davidson, C:
*A Woman's Work is Never Done -
a History of Housework in the British Isles
1650-1950,*
Chatto & Windus (1982).

Fletcher-Watson, J:
Inside a Victorian House,
National Trust (1993).

Fowler, J & Cornforth, J:
English Decoration in the Eighteenth Century,
Barrie & Jenkins (1978).

Gee, A:
Looking at Houses,
Batsford (1983).

Girouard, M:
The Victorian Country House,
Yale (1971).

Girouard, M:
The Country House Companion,
Guild Publishing (1987).

Girouard, M:
Life in the English Country House,
Yale (1977).

Honey, A:
Investigating the Victorians,
National Trust (1993).

Jackson-Stops, G:
The Country House in Perspective,
Pavilion (1990).

Keith, C:
A Teacher's Guide to Using Listing Buildings,
English Heritage (1991).

Lummis, T & Marsh, J:
The Woman's Domain,
Viking (1990).

McKinley, R R:
'The adoption of an evidence-based
approach to a site visit: a case-study',
Teaching History 38 (1984), 17-21.

Palmer, J:
'The use of Hagley Hall by a class
of junior school pupils',
Environmental Education 15 (1981), 20-23.

Paston-Williams, S:
The Art of Dining,
National Trust (1993).

Pevsner, N:
An Outline of European Architecture,
Penguin (1961).

Phillips, P:
'One man's view of teaching Tudor
domestic life',
Heritage Interpretation 26 (1984), 10-11.

Reed, M:
The Georgian Triumph,
RKP (1983).

Rowley, T: *The Norman Heritage,*
RKP (1983).

Sharpe, J A:
*Early Modern England - A Social History
1550-1760,* Edward Arnold (1987).

Summerson, J:
Architecture in Britain 1530-1830,
Penguin (1991).

Taylor C & Allwash J: 'A castle in the
classroom',
Teaching History 26 (1980), 6-8.

Thornton, P:
*Seventeenth-century Interior Decoration in
England, France and Holland,*
Yale (1978).

Tinniswood, A:
Historic Houses of the National Trust,
National Trust (1993).

Photo-credits

1 NTPL/Andreas von Einsiedel; 3 NT, NTPL/Tim Stephens; 4 Kim Williams; 5 NTPL/Roy Westlake; 7 NTPL/Matthew Antrobus; NTPL/Alasdair Ogilvie; 8-9 Toucan Books; 10 Country Life; 11 NT; 12 NTPL/L A Sparro; 13 NTPL/Andrew Butler, NTPL/George Wright; 14 NTPL/Brian Lawrence, NTPL/Mike Williams, NTPL/Nick Meers; 16 NTPL/Alasdair Ogilvie; 17 NT/Nicholas Toyne; NTPL/Alasdair Ogilvie, NTPL/Geoff Morgan, Viv van den Toorn; 20 NT; 21 NTPL/Angelo Hornak; 23 NTPL/Andreas von Einsiedel, NTPL/J Pipkin, NTPL/John Bethell; 25 NTPL/Hawkley Studios, Toucan Books; 26 NTPL/John Bethell, NTPL/Rupert Truman, NTPL/Matthew Antrobus; 27 NTPL/Rupert Truman, NTPL/William R Davis; 28 NTPL/Andreas von Einsiedel; 29 NTPL/George Wright, NTPL/Mike Williams; 30 NTPL/James Mortimer, NTPL/Andreas von Einsiedel; 31 NT, NTPL; 32 NTPL/Derrick E Whitty; 33 NTPL/Nick Meers, NTPL/George Wright; 34 NTPL/Stephen Robson; 35 NT, NTPL/Peter Aprahamian; 36 NTPL/Erik Pelham; 37 NTPL/Tim Stephens, NTPL/Andy Williams; 38 NTPL/Rupert Truman; 39 NTPL/Mike Williams; 40-1 Toucan Books; 42 NTPL/John Hammond; 43 NTPL, NTPL/P A Burton; 44 NTPL/Richard Pink; 45 NTPL/Joe Cornish, NTPL, Courtauld Institute; 46 NTPL/Eric Crichton; 47 NTPL/Andreas von Einsiedel, NTPL/Oliver Benn, NTPL/Rupert Truman; 48 NTPL/J Whitaker; 49 NT, NTPL/Alasdair Ogilvie; 50-1 Toucan Books; 52 NTPL/Nick Meers; 53 NTPL/Bill Batten; 54 NTPL/Rupert Truman; 55 Courtesy of the Board of Trustees of the Victoria and Albert Museum; 57 NTPL/Bill Batten; 58 NTPL/Andreas von Einsiedel; 59 NTPL/Bill Batten; 60 NT/Chris Hill; 62 NTPL/John Hammond; 63 NTPL/Rupert Truman, NTPL/Peter Aprahamian; 64 NTPL/Derrick E Whitty; 65 NTPL/Nick Meers, NTPL/Bill Batten; 66 NTPL/A C Cooper; 67 NTPL/Nick Meers, NTPL/Jerry Harpur; 68-9 Toucan Books; 70 NTPL/Angelo Hornak; 71 NTPL/Bill Batten, NTPL/Andreas von Einsiedel; 72 NTPL/Mark Fiennes; 73 NTPL/Christopher Hurst, NTPL; 74 NTPL/Tony Evans; 75 NT/Pieterse-Davison International, NTPL/Andrew Haslam, NTPL/Andreas von Einsiedel; 76 NTPL/Andreas von Einsiedel; 77 NT, NTPL/Andreas von Einsiedel; 78-9 Toucan Books; 80 NTPL/Andreas von Einsiedel, NTPL/Matthew Antrobus; 82 NTPL/Andreas von Einsiedel; 83 NTPL, NTPL/John Bethell; 85 NTPL/Mike Caldwell, NTPL, NT; 86 NTPL/John Bethell; 87 NTPL/Andreas von Einsiedel, NTPL/Geoffrey Frosh, NTPL/Andreas von Einsiedel; 88 NTPL; 89 NTPL/Andreas von Einsiedel; 90 NT; 91 NTPL; 92 NTPL/Chris Gascoigne; 93 NTPL/James Mortimer, NTPL/John Hammond

Body text in 9pt Janson Text with headlines and sub-heads in Bodoni Bold.

Index